BLACK SUMMER

AF865009

BLACK SUMMER

Stories of loss, courage and community by ABC journalists on the ground during the 2019–2020 bushfires

Edited by Michael Rowland

ABC BOOKS

The ABC 'Wave' device is a trademark of the Australian Broadcasting Corporation and is used under licence by HarperCollins*Publishers* Australia.

HarperCollins*Publishers*
Australia • Brazil • Canada • France • Germany • Holland • Hungary
India • Italy • Japan • Mexico • New Zealand • Poland • Spain • Sweden
Switzerland • United Kingdom • United States of America

First published in Australia in 2021
by HarperCollins*Publishers* Australia Pty Limited
Level 13, 201 Elizabeth Street, Sydney NSW 2000
ABN 36 009 913 517
harpercollins.com.au

Copyright in the individual stories remains the property of their authors (see page 325).
Compilation Copyright © Australian Broadcasting Corporation 2021
Foreword Copyright © Ita Buttrose 2021
Foreword Copyright © Andrew Constance 2021
A Season Like No Other Copyright © Michael Rowland 2021

The moral rights of the authors of this work have been asserted by them in accordance with the *Copyright Amendment (Moral Rights) Act 2000.*

This work is copyright. Apart from any use as permitted under the *Copyright Act 1968*, no part may be reproduced, copied, scanned, stored in a retrieval system, recorded, or transmitted, in any form or by any means, without the prior written permission of the publisher.

A catalogue record for this book is available from the National Library of Australia.

ISBN 978 0 7333 4132 8 (paperback)
ISBN 978 1 4607 1313 6 (ebook)

Cover design by Mark Campbell, HarperCollins Design Studio
Front cover image: Firefighters containing fires on Mount Tootie Rd, Bilpin NSW, during the January 2020 bushfires (ABC Image/Brendan Esposito)
Back cover image: Philip Williams surveying the approaching Namadgi fire from Michelago, NSW (ABC Image/Greg Nelson)
Typeset in Baskerville MT Regular by Kirby Jones
Printed and bound in Australia by McPherson's Printing Group
The papers used by HarperCollins in the manufacture of this book are a natural, recyclable product made from wood grown in sustainable plantation forests. The fibre source and manufacturing processes meet recognised international environmental standards, and carry certification.

Dedicated to everyone affected by the fires

Contents

Foreword

Ita Buttrose

THEY WERE THE MOST DEVASTATING BUSHFIRES IN LIVING memory. Australia's 2019–20 Black Summer fires burnt an estimated 18 million hectares, greater than the combined area affected by Victoria's 2009 Black Saturday bushfires and its 1983 Ash Wednesday fires.

Thirty-three people died and more than 5900 buildings were destroyed, including 3000 homes. At least one billion animals were killed and some endangered species may have been driven to extinction.

The scale and severity of the fires shocked us. We marvelled at the bravery of firefighters and other bushfire emergency responders, who risked everything to save people's lives and homes.

Our catastrophic bushfires stunned the world. The *New York Times* headlined one story: 'Australia is burning' and told its readers that, since the bushfire season started in September 2019, every state of Australia had been touched by fire. Prince Charles described the bushfires as 'an apocalyptic vision of hell'.

Throughout the summer, the ABC played a critical role in keeping people safe, with our teams in rural and regional communities working around the clock to make sure crucial information was available to people in danger from the fires. They were on the ground in almost all the fire zones and communities, conducting emergency broadcasting to disseminate crucial and, at times, lifesaving information.

Emergency broadcasting is a high-pressure job, requiring expert filtering and prioritising of information from fire and emergency services, government authorities, community organisations and listeners, who are often calling in from dangerous, stressful and unpredictable situations.

There were times during the Black Summer bushfires when the lives of our reporters were at risk and there were concerns for their safety and mental wellbeing. While nothing compares to the anguish of people who were directly affected by the fires, our teams witnessed heartbreaking human tragedy and it would have been impossible not to be impacted in some way.

But like all of us who work at the ABC, these reporters know that Australians rely on the national broadcaster in times of crisis. As 702 Sydney *Drive* host Richard Glover said, 'Everyone feels it's a privilege to be able to help in any way they can.' Richard returned from holiday leave to deliver emergency

ABC camera operator Peter Drought at Colo, NSW. (Lily Mayers/ABC)

broadcasting services. Many ABC staff did the same. *Q+A* host Hamish Macdonald was holidaying on the New South Wales south coast, one of the worst-affected areas, and began broadcasting from Bega on multiple ABC platforms and hosting live news coverage.

'We've had a great deal of feedback from people saying how reassured they felt hearing local voices on the radio, people they knew,' Lisa Markham, the chief of staff at ABC South East New South Wales, said, 'and that they appreciated hearing us on air 24 hours a day during the fires.'

There were times when the voice of the ABC was the only one people heard. 'Many people told us that,' recalled Simon Lauder, ABC South East New South Wales *Breakfast* host, who presented rolling emergency radio coverage alongside producer Jen Hunt. 'I had people in tears come up to me in the supermarket saying we saved their lives. I don't think I did anything lifesaving, but information can save lives. I feel strongly the ABC has to maintain that depth within the regions to keep doing emergency broadcasting. Living in a region makes you care a lot more than someone who doesn't. You face the people who listen to you every day. There's much at stake and you are really invested.'

Black Summer: Stories of loss, courage and community from the 2019–2020 bushfires details how the ABC's metro news rooms and local radio stations kept the nation up to date with the unfolding disaster, and reinforces the commitment and professionalism of the people who were at the frontline of our emergency broadcasting. The stories give unforgettable insights into people's fears during and after the fires, as well as their extraordinary resilience and optimism. They also paint a picture of people's kindness to others. Take, for example, Zalmai Khatiz, an Afghani migrant who has lived in Australia for forty years. He and his family stopped trying to save their own home from the flames in order to give their elderly neighbours a helping hand protecting their house. Zalmai said he wanted to give back, to show his gratitude to Australia for giving him a future.

There are horrific stories of cars with aluminium features melted into a puddle. Many tell of the horrifying 'roar' of the fires. Louise Brown lost her home, but not her Cobargo bookshop, which survived the fire that ripped through the town's main street. She announced the reopening of the shop with a sign in the window: 'Post-apocalyptic fiction now moved to current affairs.' Even amid devastation, our unique Aussie humour makes people smile. Where would we be without it?

Black Summer has been edited by ABC *News Breakfast* co-host Michael Rowland, who reported on the fires on the north and south coasts of New South Wales. As he points out in his introduction, the costs of Australia's Black Summer are still being counted. And he asks the question on many people's minds: will we never again be able to relax during summer?

Time will tell. But if indeed that is to be our fate, the ABC, as Australia's national broadcaster, will be ready to fulfil its emergency broadcasting obligations to keep Australians informed and safe. It's what they expect us to do.

Ita Buttrose, AC, OBE
Chair – Australian Broadcasting Corporation

Foreword

Andrew Constance

Life changed when the firestorms struck our community over the Black Summer of 2019–20. Mentally we are scarred forever, left with the images of what we have lost – loved ones, homes, businesses and livelihoods – and scenes we will never forget despite wanting to. Our hearts are blackened and in many cases broken. But our resolve to get through one of Australia's largest natural disasters has brought out countless community heroes. I am proud to know so many wonderful people who went above and beyond to help their families, friends, neighbours and communities.

We all drew incredible strength from our firefighters. Our New South Wales Rural Fire Service (RFS) volunteers, under the leadership of Commissioner Shane Fitzsimmons, not only put out fires and saved lives and property, but motivated and inspired the rest of the community to be the best they could be in such dark and troubled times. Together we were united in survival and together we are united in recovery.

—

I live near Batemans Bay. The smoke was like fog most days in December 2019, and my neighbours and I wondered when the fire would strike our homes. It wasn't a case of if, but when. On 31 December our turn came. New Year's Eve will never again be celebrated like it was before. From now on, it will be a day of remembrance.

At 3 am I was woken by an alert from the Fires Near Me app warning people to shelter in place. I knew the far south coast of New South Wales was in dire trouble. With no humidity and a temperature of 32 degrees before the sun had even risen, it wasn't going to be long before thousands of people would be staring death in the face from a fire that had been burning in the ranges for over a month. Unusually it wasn't a late-afternoon fire fanned by strong northwesterlies; it was a morning fire on a huge front. Small communities were under serious threat. Villages like Cobargo, Mogo, Malua Bay and Quaama would soon become etched in the nation's consciousness and ultimately embraced in the nation's kindness.

The fire I experienced was like a bomb. It hit my local community around 10 am and as it came over the hills it let off such radiant heat I thought I was going to melt and perish.

Bushfire approaching the Southern Highlands town of Penrose, NSW.
(Brendan Esposito/ABC)

The roar of the flames in the tinder-dry bushland made me very aware of my own mortality. The speed with which the fire ripped through the bush left many people feeling helpless. No one could stop it. No aircraft bomber, no fire truck, no firefighter. Only the ocean put an end to its destruction and misery.

Standing alone, confronting a firestorm on your own property, is an experience words cannot describe. You know your life is in the balance. Your first regret is that you're still there. Your home and personal belongings become somewhat irrelevant when a firestorm is a couple of hundred metres away. It's no place to be unless you are well-equipped and have experienced a bushfire before.

So in a last-minute decision, I fled to the beach at Malua Bay as the fire front tore through. What I witnessed on that beach with over a thousand other people was incredible bravery and kindness from our surf life savers, and extraordinary courage from off-duty police and highway patrol officers. Not one life was lost in Malua Bay, when realistically hundreds of us should have perished.

We had fires burning in our region for almost fifty days. So many of our firefighters lost their own homes while saving the lives and homes of others. Yet these heroes didn't give up. Having lost their home one day, they returned to fight fires the next. Day after day the brave women and men of the RFS worked in the extreme heat of those enormous fires and never once sought gratitude.

Volunteer recovery centres popped up in local showgrounds, surf clubs and community halls. The big debates on climate change and land management were irrelevant to people who were traumatised and grateful to be alive. Visits by politicians didn't mean a thing when people were scrambling to find food and shelter for themselves and their loved ones. January 2020 for us was about survival and we came together as community should, to look out for each other and show love, kindness and support.

I wish I could say that we are building towards the greatest recovery the country has ever seen following a natural disaster. But between politics and the Covid-19 virus, the realisation of that aspiration is currently delayed.

I am scared about the mental health impact of these fires and the post-traumatic stress these events have caused for so many Australians. Trauma can lead to severe depression for some people – and unfortunately for me I fall into that category. It's a painstaking and very lonely journey coming to terms with the New Year's Eve 2019 firestorms. However, like so many others, I draw strength from my community and the green shoots of recovery nurtured by those who deeply care.

Andrew Constance, MP
New South Wales Minister for Transport and Roads
Member for Bega

A Season Like No Other

Michael Rowland

It was the summer when all the holiday rituals were turned on their head. Those sleepy beachside towns to which so many Australians escape over the Christmas break were transformed from places of rest and relaxation into cauldrons of horror. Instead of spending their days searching for the perfect wave or a spot for the sunshade, holidaymakers and locals alike found themselves desperately seeking out evacuation centres as the flames edged closer, or in some instances roared towards them. Local beaches went from havens of summer fun to places of refuge as the skies darkened and the embers flew.

The 2019–20 Australian summer season was like none other this country had yet endured, thanks to the sheer scale and reach of the infernos. By its end, 33 people had died and just over 3000 homes had been destroyed. More than 18 million hectares of land in southern Australia was burnt, greater than the combined area that went up in flames in the 2009 Black Saturday fires and the 1983 Ash Wednesday blazes. Millions of Australians were affected by hazardous smoke and the bushfires killed an estimated one billion animals.

But the damage went beyond that. The fires badly singed Prime Minister Scott Morrison's reputation, as he made – and then struggled to overcome – some serious missteps while the crisis was unfolding. The catastrophe also catapulted climate change, and Australia's role in it, to the heart of political debate.

Covering the fires was a massive effort for the ABC. We made 953 emergency broadcasts over the season, compared with 371 the year before and 256 in 2017–18. Journalists, camera crews, radio presenters, producers and studio staff all hurled themselves into the job of covering the blazes and providing to the public vital information that undoubtedly saved lives.

My coverage from the fire ground began in early November on the mid-north coast of New South Wales for *News Breakfast* and the wider ABC News network. I was back in action again from New Year's Eve on the state's south coast during those dreadful days when exhausted fire crews were fearing the worst.

It is easy to forget that this fire season actually began deep in the winter of 2019. Warmer than usual conditions, combined with a drought that had left the bush tinder dry, sparked fires on the New South Wales mid-north coast and in the Hunter region as early as July. The New South Wales Rural Fire

Service (RFS) brought forward the start of the bushfire danger period for large parts of the state to 1 August, two months ahead of schedule.

The danger quickly escalated. Fires burnt all through September but it wasn't until the afternoon of Friday, 8 November that it became clear this season was going to be very different from the others. As 90 fires burnt across New South Wales – 14 at emergency warning level – a grim-faced RFS Commissioner Shane Fitzsimmons stepped up to deliver some sobering news.

'Unfortunately, we are in uncharted territory this afternoon,' he said. 'We have never seen this many fires concurrently at emergency warning levels.'

On the following Monday, catastrophic fire warnings were issued for the next day in Sydney and the Hunter, Illawarra and Shoalhaven regions. It was the first time the catastrophic rating had been used since it was introduced in 2009. A state of emergency was declared and hundreds of schools closed.

It had been an equally challenging spring in Queensland too. Homes were destroyed in Mareeba, in the north of the state, as well as in the Gold Coast hinterland, and in Stanthorpe on the Southern Downs. Samantha Wantling, a Stanthorpe local, told the ABC that the fast-approaching fire front was like 'an atomic bomb going off'. Compounding the difficulty of trying to contain the fires was a scarcity of water, thanks to the prolonged drought. Local dams and reservoirs were all but empty.

Taken by Peter Somerville, ABC Gippsland.

On 8 September, the heritage-listed Binna Burra Lodge in the Lamington National Park was razed. It had stood for 86 years.

Then in November, Port Lincoln on South Australia's Eyre Peninsula came under threat from an out-of-control fire burning on the town's fringes. Eleven houses on the Lower Yorke Peninsula were destroyed or damaged as strong winds and searing temperatures whipped up a bushfire believed to have been caused by a faulty power transformer.

By the middle of November, six people had died and more than 400 homes had been destroyed since the start of the season. Summer was still a fortnight away.

As Christmas approached, much of the country was aflame. In Western Australia, a large fire had torn though an area north of Perth, prompting evacuation orders. Parts of Tasmania were hit as well.

And still the worst was to come.

On Thursday, 19 December, volunteer firefighters Andrew O'Dwyer and Geoffrey Keaton were killed when their fire truck rolled off the road after being hit by a falling tree near Buxton, southwest of Sydney. They were working to contain the Green Wattle Creek fire. Both were fathers of young children.

Their deaths prompted the prime minister to cut short a family holiday in Hawaii, a trip that had been shrouded in puzzling secrecy by his office. PM Scott Morrison said he deeply regretted any offence his break had caused Australians affected by the bushfire crisis – but, as he saw it, there was little he could practically do.

'I don't hold a hose, mate, and I don't sit in a control room,' he told John Stanley on Sydney radio station 2GB. The PM also said he wouldn't be 'panicked' into taking stronger action to limit Australia's greenhouse gas emissions to help combat climate change. He acknowledged the link between climate change and bushfires, but said it 'wasn't credible' to link any specific fires to global warming.

—

There was no respite over the Christmas holidays for those who were actually holding the hoses. On 22 December, the Cudlee Creek fire in the Adelaide Hills destroyed 72 homes and left one man dead.

By late December, a flashpoint had emerged in the beautiful East Gippsland area of Victoria, a popular summer holiday location. Thousands of visitors and residents were ordered to leave immediately. Fifteen-thousand square kilometres were deemed to be under threat of fire. The roads out of the area filled quickly as people scrambled to leave.

On New Year's Eve, as the City of Sydney controversially went ahead with its annual harbour fireworks display, massive blazes were tearing up the New South Wales south coast. In a horrific 48 hours, seven people were killed and nearly 200 homes lost, almost half of them in the picturesque hamlet of Lake Conjola. Walking through the area a day later, I could see just how quickly the flames had taken hold and how random the destruction was. Opposite rows of destroyed houses were homes barely touched by the inferno. On the lake, holidaymakers were going about their daily business.

The historic Bega Valley town of Cobargo was also hit hard; its main street virtually wiped out. Father and son Robert and Patrick Salway died trying to defend their property at Wandella, about ten kilometres from town.

On 2 January, Scott Morrison travelled to Cobargo to offer support to some of those affected by the blaze. It was another summer trip he probably regrets. Camera crews captured the prime minister awkwardly grabbing and shaking the hand of a woman after she had refused to greet him. Mr Morrison got a similarly cool reception from a local firefighter. 'I don't really want to shake your hand,' the man said, even as the prime minister reached down to shake his left hand. An incident controller told the prime minister afterwards that the firefighter had lost his house. Later in the day, Mr Morrison was also heckled by some angry local residents who told him he wasn't welcome in Cobargo.

The prime minister wasn't the only politician running the gamut of public emotions. Also on 2 January, outside the Batemans Bay evacuation centre, I spoke to a clearly traumatised Andrew Constance, the New South Wales transport minister and MP for Bega, who had spent New Year's Eve helping fight a fire that was threatening his home in nearby Malua Bay. His home survived; some of his neighbours' homes weren't so lucky. As I asked him how he felt about the fast-climbing number of homes lost in the current bushfire crisis, Mr Constance broke down on camera.

'It's unfair,' he said. 'I met four RFS guys yesterday who lost their homes. Beautiful neighbours of mine lost their homes. It's tough. We'll get it together. We are tough here and pretty resilient people. We've been through a lot. We will recover, but it's just hard.'

—

As the New South Wales south coast was picking up the pieces, the situation in the small East Gippsland town of Mallacoota remained hairy. With the area ringed by fire and access roads cut off, 4000 locals and holidaymakers were still huddled on the beach, prepared to clamber on to the oyster-covered breakwall if the flames came any closer. On 3 January, a massive sea evacuation swung into action. Under orange skies, residents and holidaymakers boarded the navy vessels HMAS *Choules* and MV *Sycamore*. Hundreds of homes were lost in Victoria's east and northeast.

Also in early January, the fires sweeping across Kangaroo Island in South Australia took a serious turn. A third of the popular tourist location was burning and on Saturday,

4 January, the bodies of bush pilot Dick Lang and his surgeon son Clayton were found on the Playford Highway in the middle of the island. Both men had been helping to fight the fires.

As January clocked over to February, the immediate danger passed. More benign weather conditions, including a welcome dumping of rain over most of the fire grounds, brought immense relief to the fire crews on the frontline and to the communities living in constant fear of being destroyed. On 3 March, the New South Wales RFS announced that for the first time since July 2019, there were no active bush or grass fires in the state. The 240 days of fire activity had come to an end.

But the costs of Australia's black summer are still being counted. The families and friends of those who died are mourning loved ones who will never return. Those who lost their houses and all of their possessions are going through the arduous task of rebuilding their lives. The beautiful coastal and country towns that rely on the tourist dollar are dealing with the impact of the lost revenue from a summer cruelly interrupted. The coronavirus pandemic has dealt these communities another blow, making it even harder to attract the visitors back.

I urge all Australians, if you can, please make it a priority to visit these places. The people of Bermagui, Mallacoota, Kangaroo Island and many places in between would dearly love to see you.

—

The prime minister was counting the cost of his perceived inaction as the bushfires engulfed the country. Then Covid struck, allowing him to rebuild his reputation as a leader taking charge in a crisis. His government, though, is still grappling with the changing sentiment of Australian voters, an increasing number of whom believe the bushfires were a startling wake-up call to this country to do much more to tackle climate change.

And, finally, all of us have been left wondering whether the great Australian summer, and those languid days by the beach without a care in the world, will forever be a lot less relaxed.

In the coming pages you will read about the on-the-ground experiences of my ABC colleagues as they reported on fires stretching from southern Queensland, through New South Wales and eastern Victoria to Kangaroo Island in South Australia. These are, at times, deeply personal reflections as even the most hardened reporters were caught up in the raging emotions inflamed by this summer from hell.

Many of the stories are harrowing. But it is important that we honour and remember what happened and what was lost.

Michael Rowland

Co-presenter of ABC News Breakfast

UNPRECEDENTED

‘Grab the children, just grab the children.’

The firefighter’s directive played over and over in my head. It was not meant to be like this – we were meant to be celebrating. It was summertime in beautiful Bermagui. But everything was wrong. Homes were burning and people were dying.

It was the early hours of New Year’s Eve, 2019. My phone pinged at 1.30 am, waking me and my partner, Yannis. It was the Fires Near Me app.

I opened the alert and my first instinct was that there must have been a mistake. A gigantic black prong was jutting out from the map of the Badja Forest Road fire, seemingly growing larger by the minute and heading straight towards our house, our business, our community and our friends. It was beelining for our beloved Bermagui.

There was barely a breath of wind on the coast and it was the middle of the night – how could a fire be moving so quickly? Surely it was a mistake.

Yannis and I turned on the scanner to listen in to what the local firefighters were saying on their radios – it’s a tool I frequently use as a journalist to get the true picture of what’s happening on a fire ground. In just a couple of minutes it became overwhelmingly clear that the map was accurate. Adrenaline kicked in. I could feel my pulse in my temples and a knot was forming in my stomach. Yannis owns the pub in town, so we’d been hoping for a good night’s sleep before the busiest night of the year. But that was not going to happen now.

We jumped out of bed. We were not ready for this. Despite my experience of reporting on bushfires and having received several warnings from authorities already that summer, we had not packed our bags. We had not prepared our house.

We were lucky to live on a 10-hectare bush property ten minutes south of Bermagui. Tall trees, mainly spotted gums, surround the house, the leaf litter needs constant clearing – and we had dropped the ball.

We looked at each other like deer in the headlights. Could this really be happening? I dashed around the house, chucking belongings into washing baskets and filling up our cars with stuff.

Over the following hour, the intensity of the chatter on the scanner picked up rapidly. The fire was moving southeast with unapologetic ferocity through the towns of Yowrie, Tinpot and Wandella – and was heading for Verona, Quaama and Cobargo. We heard dozens of requests from firefighters, asking Firecom for more support. But none was available and none was coming. It was just local brigades trying to achieve the unachievable.

I was starting to go crazy with panic. Did I need to pack towels? Did I need to pack socks? What about my expensive knives and my great uncle's wine glasses? We were pacing around the house.

The clock ticked over to 3 am. I had to do something. I texted Cheryl McCarthy, the secretary of the Bermagui Surf Life Saving Club where I volunteer, to offer my help and she responded that the surf club had just been opened as a temporary evacuation centre. Yannis was out waking up our neighbours and making phone calls to friends close by. When he returned, I kissed him goodbye, grabbed some food supplies and raced into town to lend a hand.

I remember driving the ten kilometres into Bermagui and wondering if our house would be there when I got back. I remember thinking it was odd that all my neighbours' lights were on even though it was the middle of the night. I remember watching out for kangaroos along the road – normally in their hundreds – but there wasn't an animal in sight.

And I remember thinking that nothing would ever be the same again.

Claire Wheaton
During 2019 and 2020, Claire covered the bushfires and bushfire recovery for the ABC

The Smell of Smoke

Erin Semmler

It was the morning of the hottest November day of 2019 in Yeppoon, so naturally I was at the beach. Our coastal town of around 19,000 people, north of Rockhampton, was enjoying a glorious start to the weekend, a picture-perfect Saturday. The water was crystal blue and the sunlight glimmered on the glass-like ocean. There was not a cloud in the sky. This time of year is usually warm – according to the Bureau of Meteorology the average maximum for November is 27.6 degrees. On this day, however, the maximum temperature soared to 34.9 degrees. The winds were south-southwesterly, meaning hot, dry air was blowing into town from the west.

I left the beach around lunchtime and drove north along the esplanade towards my parents' home at Barlows Hill, on the other side of Yeppoon. I saw a plume of smoke to the west and thought it was unusual, but it didn't ring any alarm bells. It should have.

In August 2019, the Bushfire and Natural Hazards Cooperative Research Centre (CRC) had released its bushfire outlook for the coming summer, drawing on expert advice from across Australia and New Zealand. It warned communities from Rockhampton to the New South Wales border to be prepared for a long and 'very active' fire season. Weather experts said the outlook was 'not a good news story'. Around the same time this report was released, fires had already threatened homes on Bribie Island on Queensland's Sunshine Coast, north of Brisbane and Noosa.

Just before 1 pm, the Queensland Fire and Emergency Services (QFES) put out a warning for the Cobraball bushfire burning about 12 kilometres west of Yeppoon. It was a 'prepare to leave' warning, asking the public to be aware of a fast-moving grass fire and deteriorating conditions. As a journalist, my ears pricked up, but I still assumed it would be taken care of and the warning would soon be downgraded.

Leading into the weekend, the QFES had warned of severe fire danger conditions in central Queensland. They knew the winds would be strong. Given the drought conditions across the region, there was also plenty of fuel around to burn. There was no fire ban in place but authorities had firefighting aircraft on standby in Rockhampton, Gladstone and Emerald. Before the weekend, authorities were primarily concerned about the Central Highlands rather than coastal central Queensland. Despite these warnings and obvious preparation by authorities, no one thought lives and homes would be threatened. Like so many communities, we didn't think it could happen to us.

From my parents' home, I watched the plume of smoke grow bigger, darker and closer. Half an hour after the first warning, a 'leave now' order was issued for Cobraball. It read, 'the fire could have a significant impact on the community'. It was not a warning that evacuated my parents and me, or the densely populated areas of Yeppoon, but the real threat to lives had my heart racing.

The wind was gusty and the smoke blanketed the sun, leaving an ominous red sphere in place of its usual golden glow. That afternoon, the first evacuation centre was opened at the basketball courts in Yeppoon. As night fell, the plume of smoke expanded and turned into what looked like a sea of red lava. My hometown was burning.

The first emergency level warning was issued just after 7 pm. I tried to help the only way I knew how, by keeping the community informed using our local ABC Capricornia Facebook page. Being a small town, everyone knew someone threatened by the out-of-control flames. I shared as many photos, words, warnings and announcements on social media as I could – interacting with our audience who began to share their own experiences in the comments. Cars towing caravans and horse floats lined the roads of Yeppoon – not a usual sight for a Saturday night.

In less than 24 hours, two fire fronts joined together and burnt more than 6000 hectares of bush, grazing and agricultural land. Authorities described the night's emergency as an 'unprecedented event'. At its peak, the fire was 14 kilometres long, six kilometres wide and burning on multiple fronts.

Amid the chaos, a disaster declaration was made for the area and police went door to door to warn hundreds of residents who were in the path of the raging fire. Two residents on the list for a visit by the police were Greg and Petria Stack, who lived in Bungundarra, in the hinterland to the northwest.

Unaware of the unfolding emergency, that evening the couple had sat down for dinner as usual. They had no idea the fire – which had started about 15 kilometres south of their property earlier in the day – was on their doorstep. The flames had reached them faster than the authorities. 'By the time they got here, it was just too late,' Greg told me later.

'Our son rang us and told us it was at the top of our hill; his friend told him,' Petria recalled. 'We just didn't know. We went outside and looked up the top of the hill and a big fireball was coming down. I said, "We've got to get out, we've got to go." So we just left. It was frightening the way it was coming down the hill. It was so quick and ferocious that we didn't even have time to think.'

Greg and Petria Stack outside the remains of their home in Bungundarra, Queensland. (Erin Semmler)

Without a minute to spare, the couple got in their car with the clothes on their backs, a pair of glasses, a laptop, a handbag and medication. They stopped at the bottom of their driveway and watched as the flames engulfed decades of memories. 'We parked down on the road and watched it all burn,' Petria said. 'We were just so much in shock we didn't know what to do. We just sat there for a while.'

—

They were not the only ones caught by surprise by the Cobraball-Bungundarra fire. QFES state coordinator Neil Francis said many properties came 'under ember attack' during Saturday night, making conditions extremely difficult for fire crews.

Mark Taylor, an RFS volunteer, had been out fighting the fire on a different front when his wife, Jenny, called and told him it had reached their property at Bungundarra. 'They were saying there's embers dropping and the front drive was already on fire then,' Mark explained later to me and my ABC colleague Megan Hendry. He told Jenny to call triple zero and then raced home.

Through the thick smoke, firefighters responding to the call evacuated Jenny, her mother and father, her teenage son and their puppy in a fire truck, before transferring them into a waiting ambulance. By then Mark had arrived and had decided to stay with firefighters to defend the property. 'I didn't see them go,' Mark told me, of his family's evacuation. 'We were over in the corner, protecting that part of the house. I knew they were in good hands.'

The Taylors' dark-brick house was damaged by the flames but not destroyed. But a shed and granny flat they had just finished building for Jenny's father was reduced to a pile of rubble. Like other rural firefighting volunteers, over the following hours and days, Mark continued to fight the fire wherever he was needed.

—

At my parents' place, I had little sleep. On Sunday morning, winds continued to fan the flames. I had asked my dad the night before if he thought my aunty and uncle's Woodbury property, northeast of Bungundarra, would be under threat. Dad told me I was overreacting.

It was just after five o'clock in the morning when I heard the phone ring. My aunty and uncle, Diana and Rob, had just been told by police that it was a good idea to activate their bushfire survival plan and evacuate. The winds were forecast to change direction and push the erratic blaze east towards their Woodbury home by lunchtime. My dad and I changed into boots, long-sleeved shirts and long pants while Mum brewed us coffee, then off we went. As we drove north along Farnborough

Road, billows of smoke lingered to the west of the mountains. I'd never seen anything like it.

The same green rolling hills I had driven past so many times as a child were now brown, and the normally blue sky behind the hills was full of smoke. I could feel the adrenaline coursing through my veins – the whole thing felt surreal.

We rolled into my aunty and uncle's driveway and parked by the large shed my uncle had built a few years earlier. On the outside Uncle Rob seemed calm but I could tell by his actions he was concerned. Their caravan was packed and ready to go. They had experienced bushfires when they had lived in southern Australia so they didn't ever plan to stay and defend their home. My dad offered the space in the back of his car for any items his brother wanted to save.

I went up to the house to check on my aunty. She had filled every spare inch of her car with family photos and other sentimental items. There was still so much she wanted to pack but, in the end, she just wanted to leave before it was too late. Aunty Diana said she had always told Uncle Rob to cut the bamboo trees down near the house – they're known to explode in fires.

It was time to say goodbye, but my uncle was still shifting things into the middle of the shed. I remember he said something like, 'If I move some of the stuff away from the walls, it might not burn.'

I took a photo of the house and packed cars just before we left, thinking it could be the last time I would see their home as it was. Then we drove away from the property – Aunty Diana in her car with their Yorkshire terrier, Sapphire, Uncle Rob in their second car towing their caravan, and my dad and I following behind. Their neighbour decided he was going to stay.

Later that morning, ten aircraft and more than 50 trucks continued to fight the blaze as I raced off to work in Rockhampton, about 45 minutes' drive from my parents' home in Yeppoon. I sat at my desk for hours, as my colleague Megan Hendry, who was out speaking to people on the ground, fed me harrowing stories to share on our social media.

After my work day ended, I went with my aunty and mum to the Yeppoon community meeting outside the evacuation centre at the basketball courts. The local disaster management group told residents the fire was still out of control, but said they were hoping conditions might ease slightly overnight. Tensions were high – some people at the meeting had no idea if their homes were still standing.

That evening, my family and I went along to a close friend's birthday dinner. It felt wrong to be there. There were people at the evacuation centre worried for their homes and here I was out at a dinner party. I could tell my aunty and uncle, sitting across from me at the table, were thinking about their little home. It was so difficult to switch off. That night, I was exhausted but unable to sleep. It was still so hard to believe that while I lay in bed safe and sound, people were risking their lives to contain the blaze.

Mark Taylor and his family lost their granny flat but not their house. (Erin Semmler)

Salvation Army volunteers prepare morning tea packs for rural fire crews in Queensland's Scenic Rim. (Josh Bavas/ABC)

On Monday morning I woke to the smell of smoke. I could taste it. Still, off I went to the gym just before 6 am to maintain some routine. The smoke was thick in the main street, visibility was low. The private all-girls high school had closed its doors for the day and even postponed some Year 12 exams. Those with respiratory conditions were advised to shut their windows and doors. Even healthy people were encouraged not to exercise outdoors.

The QFES's priority on Monday was to help people return to their homes. They were able to establish some containment lines around the western front of the fire but it was not completely under control. Firies said flames had, at times, reached up to 20 metres overnight. Over the next few days crews worked tirelessly to suppress the fire.

Throughout the traumatic event, the support in the community was overwhelming. Kids wrote notes and made snack packs for firefighters and other volunteers. People donated money to feed hungry livestock. Small businesses donated clothes, food and other essential items. Everyone gave what they could, whether it was time, money or goods. Even some of those who were not sure if their homes were safe were helping others. It made me proud to call Yeppoon home.

By Thursday morning around 90 per cent of the fire was contained. The Cobraball-Bungundarra blaze ended up burning more than 11,000 hectares of land. The Department of Agriculture and Fisheries estimated $20 million worth of loss to farms in central Queensland, factoring in loss of production and damaged infrastructure. Fifteen homes were destroyed and many more structures were damaged.

—

Thankfully the wind change on Sunday did not have the impact that had been predicted and firefighters were able to stop the blaze from racing over the hill and devouring my aunty and uncle's home. They were two of the lucky ones.

Two weeks after the fire, I visited Greg and Petria Stack at their property. As I approached the location where their home had once stood, the devastation was clear. Black ash covered the landscape. I passed burnt trees, brown leaves, and structures that had been damaged and destroyed. The smell of smoke lingered.

Some homes in the area had been spared; the couple's next-door neighbours had had better luck than the Stacks. On Greg and Petria's property, the fire had missed a small shed, which had sheltered a possum and her joey from the flames. It was a symbol of hope, for a couple who had lost so much.

Greg and Petria led me up their dirt driveway, their rubber thongs crunching as we approached a piece of flattened land. The skeleton of a caravan and ride-on lawn mower sat blackened among piles of rubble. Then we came to the place where their home had once stood. The sky joined endless mountain ranges for as far as the eye could see and I understood why the couple had chosen to call the spot home some 20 years before. Now sheets of warped corrugated iron were strewn across the grey ash-filled clearing. Collector sets of salt and pepper shakers lay cracked on the concrete slab among other once-ordinary but now sentimental items. Broken glass, burnt appliances and kitchen utensils were scattered among the larger ruins. 'Seventy-two years of memorabilia is gone,' Petria said. 'It's very hard.'

Months on, the Yeppoon community remains resilient, though the fire is a scar that will never completely heal. Many more questions are being asked about bushfire preparedness in the region. Families continue to rebuild their lives. And everyone wants to make sure they will not be surprised in the same way again.

Erin Semmler is a features reporter for ABC Capricornia

The Fire Near Me

Richard Glover

It's a weird thing being in a safe radio studio when someone like Craig Tooker rings in. It was a bit after 4 pm on Saturday, 31 December, and Craig's house was surrounded on all sides by fire.

Standing at the front window of his house near Sassafras, southwest of the New South Wales coastal town of Nowra, Craig described the wall of flame that was bearing down on him. The property had been well prepared, but there was now no escape. Worse, Craig had asked his 25-year-old son to come home that day to help to protect the family house, because he had experience fighting fires; Craig now regretted that decision. He believed there was a chance they'd both perish.

'We're under attack here,' he told me, live on air. 'The bush around us is on fire, whatever we've got around the place is on fire and we're surrounded. It's like night here. We've taken refuge in the house so we're still all right but there's this enormous glow to the north of us now … you've never heard anything like it in your life, the roar, the roar. I keep saying it's like a freight train, but it's like being *under* a freight train, and all I've got is this orange glow. We've got every light in the house on because otherwise you can't see a thing. It's absolutely like midnight.'

I could hear Craig's son, Dave, in the background, agreeing with his dad's description. 'It's like a freight train,' Dave echoed.

Craig started to paint a wider picture. He'd heard one neighbour had already lost his house, and Craig was now beginning to express his fears for another. He then interrupted himself. 'Oh, look at this … we've got some big trees about 50 metres from us and they are going up now.'

We brought the call to an end. I promised to ring back.

—

During this summer of emergency broadcasts, Craig wasn't the only caller to describe terrifying moments of fire bearing down. More commonly, though, people rang to swap information.

On the night of 10 January 2020, fire was close to townships in the Blue Mountains, northwest of Sydney. A southerly wind change was expected at 10 pm. If this 'southerly buster' brought powerful gusts, the fire would be pushed towards homes. If weak, the houses would be safe. But the change was slow to arrive. We started our broadcast at 10 pm. Midnight came and went, then 1 am. Every caller to the radio, it seemed, had the same set of apprehensive questions: When would the change arrive? How strong would it be? Should I evacuate now, or wait another hour?

Finally, around 2 am, listeners further south came to the rescue. They rang the radio station, charting the progress of the southerly as it ran up the coast: first Nowra – extremely blustery – then Kiama – less strong – then Wollongong – a further weakening. By 2.45 am I was taking calls from listeners in Penrith, at the foot of the mountains. The buster had arrived but was running out of steam. It was less intense than feared, especially for those inland. A stomach-knotting night ended, a bit after 3 am, with a sigh of relief.

A month on – in mid-February – a listener called Barbara wrote to the ABC about her experience that night: the car packed, the bags beside the door, wondering whether to stay or go while they listened to the radio. She wrote: 'Richard asked people on the ground to ring in and report what they were seeing. With all that information we felt confident to stay and not evacuate, although the car was packed and ready.' As it turned out, that was the best decision. Barbara wrote to offer thanks to the presenter, but in truth the praise belonged to those ABC listeners further south, who – while staring down threats to their own lives and property – had acted on their urge to help.

—

During those stints in the studio, I found myself talking about places I'd never heard of, with unlikely names. While discussing the Gospers Mountain fire, I'd rattle off Wicketty Wees, Mount Tootie or the Vale of Clwydd. When charting the south coast fires, I'd speak with pretended familiarity about places such as Tinpot, Boggy Plain, Yankees Gap, Bumbo, Nobbies Island or Devils Hole. I'd stand in the studio, with rough maps I'd drawn by hand, trying to understand the relative positioning of the various tiny settlements. A northern wind change might be bad news for Mount Tootie, for instance, but a relief for the people of Wicketty Wees.

Then, on Saturday, 4 January, there was a place name I knew rather too well. It came accompanied by the advice: 'Under immediate threat: it is now too late to leave.' It was the location of my own house in the bush.

Decades ago, when I was in my late twenties, my partner, Debra, and I had built a mudbrick house with friends in the bush near Wombeyan Caves, northwest of Goulburn. Later, our two young sons had worked to complete the building. We still visited the house regularly, marvelling at what we, this mob of hopeless construction workers, had managed to achieve.

For weeks, I'd known there was fire in the area. Like half the state, every day began with a check of the Rural Fire Service (RFS) phone app, Fires Near Me. Each time I looked, the fire was closer to our beloved mudbrick house. My neighbours up in Wombeyan told me the fire's arrival was a case of 'when' not 'if'.

By chance, that 'when' happened while I was on air. I was hosting the emergency broadcast – interviewing mayors, power companies and reporters on the fire front, while my colleague Dom Knight assembled the information from the RFS. Every 15 minutes, Dom would arrive in the studio and present the latest official warnings.

I can still vividly remember the moment when, amid a blizzard of under-threat place names, Dom read the sentence that caught me by the throat: 'In Wombeyan Caves, the fire has now jumped Tallygang Mountain Road.'

Tallygang Mountain Road, I should explain, is not one of the state's best-known thoroughfares. This was, surely, the first time its name had ever been uttered on radio. It's a dirt track, really, alongside which there are a handful of houses.

Including ours.

—

I understand this account is jumping around in time, but I'm also aware that we've left Craig and Dave Tooker in Sassafras, staring down the fire. After Craig's call, my phone screen had filled with text messages from listeners, wishing the pair luck and desperately hoping for an update on their fate. We waited an hour, worried about distracting him from the task at hand. At around 5.15 pm, my producer, Hannah Achelles, tentatively put in the call. Craig picked up the phone, confirming he had time to talk.

The situation was still bad, he told our listeners. 'We actually saw some sky for a moment,' he said, 'and I thought, OK, we're right, but now it's gone pitch-black again and there's this ominous orange glow to the south of us. I think we've still got a lot of fire to come. I'm just looking at a tree going up now, it's about 50 metres away, and it's starting to go up into the canopy now.'

All the same, he said, things felt slightly better than they did an hour before, when the fire had first come over the ridge. At that point, Craig recalled, 'the grass was on fire. It came down like it was running. The wind was just carrying it along the ground. It was like it was alive, it was a living thing coming towards us. I've never been so frightened in my life.'

We agreed we'd ring him again, in about an hour's time.

—

That feeling of panic, so apparent in our calls with Craig, had been building for months. Even before the tragedies on the New South Wales south coast, the fires had devastated the north coast of the state and burnt through communities in New England. In central Sydney, a place normally oblivious to bushfires, the air was full of smoke. By early December, the Sydney Opera House, whose white-tiled sails normally sparkle in the sunlight, was hardly visible through the thick haze. Ferries were cancelled due to low visibility, and in offices, smoke alarms blared constantly. Schoolchildren were kept all day in their classrooms, shielded from smoke-filled playgrounds. In my own suburb, senior citizens laboured up the road to the shops, clutching hankies to their mouths.

One day, while presenting on radio, I felt so nauseous that I brought a bucket into the studio, worried I might vomit. I told my listeners about the bucket – oversharing is a hazard of my profession – and was rewarded with stories of others who'd been dry-retching in cars, bent double with asthma or felled by migraines.

The British singer Liam Gallagher, visiting Sydney for a concert, said the smoke made the city feel 'spooky'. Actually, 'biblical' might be a better word – with eerie red sunsets that looked like the end of time. It all seemed unprecedented. In fact, 'unprecedented' was that summer's recurring word. There were unprecedented fish deaths in our inland rivers; Sydney had an unprecedented level-one fire warning; every state and territory had an unprecedented day of blazes. In rural Australia, towns were reaching the end of their water supply, with no clear idea of what would happen once the taps ran dry. Meanwhile – unprecedented again – 23 former fire and emergency services leaders issued a joint statement blaming the fires on climate change and demanding the country do more to reduce greenhouse gases.

'We live as in a villa on Vesuvius,' George Bernard Shaw had written nearly a century before, and the quote seemed perfect for the times. The carefree ease of an Australian summer was gone. The sense of peril seeped in with the smoke, sliding under every doorway and through every window, filling houses with the acrid smell of burning forests. In the middle of the night, people in inner Sydney would awake to the smell of smoke, their half-asleep brains flooding their bodies with adrenaline. *The house is on fire! No, now I remember, it's the bushfires.* But, by then, the heart was pounding.

Elsewhere, of course, the house really was on fire. By the end of summer, at least a billion animals, birds and reptiles were lost in New South Wales alone. Add to that the frogs, fish, platypuses and insects not included in that figure. More than 20 per cent of Australia's forests were burnt, more than 3000 homes were lost.

And, of course, 33 Australians lost their lives.

—

Back in the studio, as the fire swept towards our mudbrick house, Dom continued his updates. When fires are at emergency level, the ABC's policy is to present updates every 15 minutes. This meant I had many opportunities to hear about Tallygang

Mountain Road – each time read in Dom's calm, professional manner. He recounted how, according to the latest RFS news, the fire was now raging on both sides of the road. I didn't say anything, of course. My place was no more important than anyone else's. Actually, it was less important than most. A weekender, rather than a home. No livestock. No one present with their life at risk.

At the end of the shift, I handed over to my radio buddy James Valentine and drove home, ultimately falling into bed and a sleepless night wondering whether our house would survive. As I lay there, anxious and sleepless, I thought about the years in which my friends, my partner, Debra, and I had made the mudbricks, shovelling wet dirt into our homemade wooden moulds. Then the years of preparing and then heaving up the frame of the building, followed by the years of clambering around at height, terrified, as we screwed down the roof. I also remembered my two young sons, working away with such gusto, becoming more completely themselves with each swing of the hammer.

And, as the night went on, I also thought about my friends who lived on the other side of that same fire. They're proper farmers, not just blockies like us. Their property is their whole life. If the wind continued blowing from the northwest, it would destroy our place. But if it turned that night and started blowing from the south, our friends would get the fire. If I had to choose, I'd rather our place was burnt than theirs.

But I don't get to choose. The wind gets to choose.

Taken by Richard Glover.

Since I couldn't sleep, I opened the app again. The perimeter of the fire had been growing for weeks, the burnt area indicated by grey hatching. Our place was now entirely within the hatched area. A week before, I'd considered driving up there, ready to defend the place, but had discounted the idea. There's only one road in. It would be easy to become stuck. I didn't have the right gear. I could put others at risk. And, courtesy of my job at the radio, I could do something vaguely useful in town. At the time I'd thought, if the place goes, it goes. Now I had my doubts.

I was safe in Sydney, but I also realised that to lose our place in the bush would be to hack away something of myself. People say, 'It's just property,' and 'You can always rebuild,' which are both true, but only in the lamest of ways. Almost any house is an accretion of memories and experiences. Houses become a physical manifestation of the most important things in your life. In my case, the adventurous spirit of my young sons; my partner's fierce determination when she wielded a chainsaw; the perpetual can-do optimism of Philip, my mate and fellow builder.

I made the building and the building made me.

In his autobiography, the Swiss psychiatrist Carl Jung wrote about a home he built on the shores of Lake Zurich. He called the building 'a kind of representation in stone of my innermost thoughts'. When the building was finished, he wrote, he was 'reborn in stone'. It doesn't sound so grand when you're building using adobe bricks – 'reborn in mud' sounds rather messy – but

I know what Jung meant. Houses are machines for living. They fast become more than rows of bricks and sheets of steel. They become part of you, through the process of building, dreaming and living. When they burn, we never forget.

—

Back on 31 December, an hour after our last conversation, it was time to put in our third call to Craig Tooker. By now it was about 6.15 pm. Again, my producer, Hannah, was nervous. We were hoping he would answer; hoping the news would be good.

Craig answered our call and the relief in his voice was immediately apparent. 'I believe it's passed through,' he told me live on air. 'We've still got a lot of smoke, but we're outside, just going down to a neighbour's house – there's fire all around his house, but he's still standing, I don't know how. So, you'd have to say, as far as this fire event goes, we seem to have survived it.'

I said we'd all been worried about the two of them.

'Rest easy now,' he replied. 'I think we're good.'

He still didn't understand how they'd been saved.

—

On the morning of 5 January – the day after I'd heard the emergency warning for Tallygang Mountain Road – I woke up and checked for news about our place. There was a message on Facebook, sent by one of my Wombeyan neighbours, Simon Chalker. Sometime around midnight, Simon and his dad, Mick Chalker, had saved our house.

'A firestorm went through there,' Simon's message read. 'We couldn't believe it when we drove in and the house was still there. We stayed for a few hours because the house was still under ember attack. The shed is still there too. You lost the top of the septic tank so be careful walking around, not a nice thing to step into!'

It was hard to express the waves of gratitude I felt.

You might imagine that, at a time like this, people would become selfish, trying to protect their own place; worrying about how their sheds and homes and stock will fare. Both on the radio and in the hills around Wombeyan Caves, I saw little evidence of that. Instead, people seemed to spend every moment worrying about someone else. By putting themselves in the way of the flames, the firefighting volunteers were the most obvious example of this spirit of generosity and community. But other examples abounded.

Take, for instance, one of my other Wombeyan neighbours, Andrea Harvey. She's a vet and has established a brumby sanctuary a few kilometres down Tallygang Mountain Road from our place so she can study their biology and behaviour. In a large paddock tucked into the hills, there's a motley crew of about 30 animals, including some newborn foals. All the locals walk up there, whenever we can, to marvel at their beauty.

When the fire first hit, it raced towards Andrea's brumbies. The local RFS brigades charged down the narrow dirt road to save them. There was smoke everywhere and some very panicked animals. The brumbies are wild, yet have become habituated to Andrea. As she emerged through the smoke and chaos, the horses saw her. Immediately they surrounded her, gathering close. She walked them to safety. As she did so, the local fire crew drove back the fire front.

That night Andrea wanted to sleep in the paddock so the horses would feel secure. The local RFS crews, with great respect, suggested that might not be sensible. She knows the crews. They know her. She accepted their wise counsel. The horses survived.

In that knot of hills, it was one story among many.

I could tell of my neighbour Peter's police officer daughter, working day and night putting out flames and drafting her new husband into service.

Or Peter himself, helping Andrea to source fresh water for the brumbies after the firefighters were forced to drain her dam.

Or the RFS brigade from Cawdor, more than 100 kilometres away, who came to fight our edge of the fire when they had their own fire front pressing down.

Or Mick, our unofficial mayor, who knows every house and every dirt track and every available water source and who had not rested since this thing began.

Or Annette, Mick's wife, a local born and bred, who accepts every newcomer into her heart. I saw her on Facebook, offering supplies, company, reassurance.

'I feel better today,' wrote Andrea on Facebook, after a day in which her horses faced new threats. 'Annette has given me a pep talk.'

Annette even knew how to make us laugh. A few days before the fire went through, the pink cricket Test had begun in Sydney. Up at Wombeyan, the aerial firefighters were bombing the area around Annette and Mick's house with their pink fire retardant. 'What a great relief,' posted Annette on Facebook, alongside a shot of the reddened landscape. 'Pink is my colour, and it was Jane McGrath Day.'

Fires leave terrible destruction in their wake, but they also leave deeper human bonds. I know that sounds trite, but I saw it happen.

One day, the bush would return. One day, the scars on the landscape would heal. But the locals would never be the same. They'd learnt something about each other. Amid the terror of the smoke and the flame, there was a new love and respect in those hills.

—

By the middle of February, the fires were beginning to subside. There were several days of very heavy rain. The smoke was washed from the air; all the fires were extinguished or contained. The main dam that supplies Sydney filled with water. In the space of days, it went from crisis level, with bans on Sydneysiders using a hose to water their garden, to at least some dams overflowing.

I decided it was time, once again, to ring Craig Hooker down in Sassafras. How was he now? How did he reflect on that terrible day? Were there green shoots – figuratively as well as literally?

Not everyone wants to talk publicly about such difficult experiences, but Craig declared himself ready. After we spoke on the radio, my text screen was busy once more. This time, though, the messages weren't filled with anxiety – just praise. 'Thank you,' said one. 'We have all benefitted so much from hearing this man's lived experience.'

What he said that day, six weeks on from the fire, was remarkable, partly because it deviated from what has become almost a media requirement: that Aussies, affected by disaster, must shrug it off with a 'No worries, we'll be right.' Craig said something different.

'There was a short period of euphoria,' he recalled, 'that happened after that event. We went back up to the house and cracked a beer each and sat down among the fires that were sort of spotting, and just toasted each other. That was the first and the last bit of euphoria we ever had as a result of that fire. Since then, it's just been the reckoning that's been coming, that's been settling on us, and the gravity of what we went through and what we experienced. It can get overwhelming at times. In your own private time you keep on going over and over it at night. You know? It doesn't drive you mad, I suppose. But it could. It could.'

—

I'd visited my own place a couple of times since the fires had swept through, surveying the damage and beginning the clean-up. As my saviour Simon Chalker had explained in his message, the lid on the septic tank had ignited and needed replacing. It didn't prove the most pleasant of jobs. A couple of our sheds had also been destroyed, along with all the fencing and an old caravan. Nothing important, in other words, and nothing to give pause to the joy we felt about the house being saved.

And, of course, a few weeks on from the fires, the rains had come. As I walked around the block in early February, I was thrilled to see full dams and overflowing tanks. But the rain, still falling, had yet to help the animals. All around the district, the kangaroos were crowding around the few remaining structures. They were thin and wet; bedraggled. The little ones, in particular, didn't run away as they normally would. There was nowhere else to go, just an endless carpet of black ash, stretching for kilometres. One tiny fellow, standing close to the back wall of our house, looked up into my camera as if to say, 'What am I meant to do now?'

The only remaining feed was located in the few metres around each building. In saving (almost every) shed or house on our dirt road, the RFS had also saved a narrow apron of drought-weary grass. It was this the kangaroos were relying on, and why they were clustered close around each isolated building. The animals worked away at what was left of the chewed-down grass and sniffed at the odd lump of sweet potato left out by locals like us.

Another weird sight: our back deck was heavy with kangaroo scats – the result, I'm guessing, of the night they sheltered close to the house as the fire pushed in from all sides. Below the deck, I spotted a wombat in residence. Its new home was not the best news for our foundations, but who was I – a member of the species who helped cause all this – to question that fellow's choice of evacuation centre?

In the wake of the fires, the gum leaves had turned white. They looked – and sounded – like paper. When the wind came through, they shook like a Japanese paper wind chime; it was the eeriest sound you can imagine. Now, five weeks since the fire raged through, the leaves had turned russet. A puff of wind would send them falling to the ground.

Australia's trees are not deciduous, right? They were now. It felt like mid-autumn in North America. Now, in early February, the rain was still heavy. In a few weeks' time, it really would be autumn, but a strange autumn that would masquerade as spring. After so much rain – about 100 millimetres in a few days – a surge of growth was coming. It's rain, especially after flame, that kindles what Dylan Thomas called 'the green fuse'.

Already, deep in the forest, a handful of trees were sprouting green, tiny leaves clustered on the trunk, luminous against the matt black of burnt bark. The tree trunks oozed a white foam, which, in the heavy rain, was driven into the streams that were running hard along the dirt track outside our place. It looked like someone had spilt a bottle of detergent. The white foam, I was later told, is a chemical compound, rich in saponins. When rain comes after drought, the eucalypts shed the chemical to help the water penetrate the dry soil around their bases.

Isn't nature wonderful?

Yes, I thought as I squelched through the muddy ash, but this is our moment of peril. We must get this right. Can we indulge our wonder in Australia's resilient nature and still hold firm to our concern and anger about climate change? Can we repeat our customary phrase, 'the bush will recover, the people will rebuild,' while also remembering the rage, panic, terror and pain of this terrible summer?

We can comfort ourselves by endlessly quoting – as our politicians love to do – the words of Dorothea Mackellar: her 'sunburnt country' of drought and flood. Or we can read Henry Lawson's poem about the Paroo, a river which, in drought, grows so insignificant that Lawson's hapless travellers step over it oblivious, but which then floods once again after rain (as it did in February 2020). Or we can chuckle over John O'Brien's 'Said Hanrahan', written in 1919, with a farmer's complaints about drought, replaced with his complaints about flood, always with the same mournful mantra: '"We'll all be rooned," said Hanrahan.'

We can comfort ourselves in this, our customary way, telling ourselves it's all normal.

But it hasn't been normal. We're back to that word again: it's been unprecedented.

Some trees will recover, some won't. Ground cover will return, but will it be in the form of weeds or native grasses? In some places, the fire burnt with such intensity that the seed bank was destroyed. Rainforests, ill-adapted to fire, may never recover.

An optimistic narrative will be hard to resist once the green shoots return. That tiny kangaroo in my back yard, too exhausted to escape my camera, will soon, I hope, be bouncing away with its mob. Human communities, I know, are already tighter, more united, bound by a million moments of bravery and kindness. Everywhere, there is bottomless gratitude for the firefighters.

And yet I hope the rains don't wash away the memories of this terrible summer. This summer should remain a line in the sand. It should remain a call to arms. It should be confirmation – if confirmation were needed – that, in a world of climate change, Australia is the canary in the mine.

The bush will (mostly) recover. The burnt towns will (mostly) be rebuilt. Our job? We must remember this fire season and the promises we made to ourselves right at that moment we were ringed by flame.

The world must change. How about now?

Richard Glover presents Drive *on ABC Radio Sydney*

DISASTER

The first ten days of 2020 were a total blur of what can only be described as apocalyptic hell. There was no power, no reception, no petrol, no medicine and dwindling food supplies. The disinfectant infrastructure at Brogo Dam had been destroyed by fire, making the water unsafe to drink.

Yannis and I spent our time madly trying to prepare our property and helping our business partners get their farm ready in case of another ember attack. We offered the pub's food supplies to the community, and generally tried to facilitate whatever needed doing in the town. We saved ourselves some prosciutto, cheese and bread from the pub and allowed ourselves one toasted sandwich per day, which we cooked on a gas cook top.

After a week, my dirty clothes were hanging off me, my nails were black with grime and all hygiene had gone out the window. When I eventually showered, it was under a cold hose with water from our dam.

I have never lived through a war, but it felt like wartime.

Claire Wheaton

A selfie in fire-safety gear.
(Claire Wheaton)

The Faces of Fire

Brittany Evins

MIDDAY WAS YET TO ARRIVE AND ALREADY I WAS WATCHING a thick, black plume of smoke pour though the main street of Lobethal, a usually peaceful Adelaide Hills township. Flames were lapping at the tops of trees, turning the sky black and red. Emergency vehicles raced through the township, past red-faced residents driving to the local oval, a designated 'bushfire-safer' place. It is one of many locations in South Australia's Adelaide Hills that the State's Country Fire Service (CFS) has identified will provide a safe refuge point for people relocating early. The closest bushfire 'last-resort' refuge – a place to use when your bushfire plan has failed – is ten minutes up the road.

It was 20 December. I had just spent the week reporting on the hot weather and dangerous conditions across South Australia and had been assigned to coordinate the content being streamed back from the fire ground in the Hills. I was watching the Lobethal fire from the safety of our Adelaide office, at least 40 minutes' drive away. The distance was anything but comforting.

At the bushfire-safer place at Balhannah Oval, some residents were arriving in cars filled with belongings. Others, like Woodside resident Annie Whicker, walked there with their horses. 'We don't hold a lot of hope,' Annie said to an ABC reporter, 'so expect that we won't have anywhere to return home.'

The CFS scanners were flooded with voices. It is a tough and all-consuming job listening to the scanners, but it is particularly important during emergency reporting, to keep abreast of the changing conditions on the fire ground. Firefighters were talking about a northerly wind change expected in the coming hours. Road closures were already put in place, and more closures were expected soon.

Then one voice cut through the babble. 'Phone towers are down, unable to get triple zero.' It was a firefighter and the tone in their voice implied something was awry. Very awry. 'Can you pass on to SAAS [South Australian Ambulance Service], we're getting multiple patients presenting at Lobethal fire station. Patient number one, 25-year-old male – he's got second-degree burns to his neck.'

Just then, as crews were protecting assets in Inverbrackie, Lobethal and Woodside, the wind changed, bringing with it lightning and hail. Power was pre-emptively cut to more than 11,000 homes.

The media helicopter started streaming back new pictures: homes burnt to the ground, and others surrounded by fire. Towns to the northeast of the blaze – Charleston, Harrogate and Mount Torrens – were now under threat and the weather conditions just kept getting worse, fuelling the hungry flames.

As the afternoon set in, the Cudlee Creek fire threatening the Adelaide Hills was still uncontrolled and burning in a northeasterly direction.

I live in the Adelaide Hills and had evacuated that morning. From the safety of my desk at work I watched the fire consume township after township as it headed towards my own home.

—

Driving towards the fire ground the next day I tuned into ABC Radio and heard an update from Balhannah Oval. Annie Whicker had just found out her worst fears had come true: she had lost everything.

'Our property is gone,' she said, live on air. 'The fires went through and have taken it all. My husband and I are here [at the refuge point] with our horse, and my daughter is here, who we have been separated from all day – so it's nice to be back together, to have some of the family here.'

Annie Whicker praised the firefighters and talked about the community who had gathered at the refuge point over the last 24 hours. 'We all had hopes and we all had different stories: "Your house is safe … but it burnt your neighbours,"' she said. 'Then the news came through that ours had gone as well. So many people have lost so much today. We run our business from home, so all our business paperwork is gone, but we're all alive and we'll have to regroup and get it together.'

The radio interview was interrupted by an emergency warning message, which anyone listening to ABC Radio around the state would have heard: 'You are in danger and you need to take action immediately, you will be impacted by fire.' Several Adelaide Hills towns were listed to be under threat. During emergencies like this, a specialised team of radio presenters are brought into ABC offices. Their role is to provide updates depending on information the CFS releases, on where the fire is and the direction it is moving. The messages, providing lifesaving information, are broadcast hourly, half-hourly, or whenever necessary depending on the fire's impact.

The funny thing about being a journalist is we rarely listen to our own broadcast advice. Instead, we head towards the danger, in the opposite direction to the steady stream of cars leaving the area – the ones listening to our advice. And so, I kept driving. I was driving towards the fire ground, but in this instance, it was for selfish reasons. I was beelining to Hahndorf, the German Adelaide Hills town where my family home would hopefully still be standing.

As night fell, I waited, like many residents, for the wind to change. The glow of fire outlined the rolling hills in the distance and turned the sky an eerie orange and a strange shade of purple. It was as if the sun was about to pop back up over the horizon. The strong smell of the burnt landscape made it hard to breathe and harder to relax.

—

Six days after the fires started, there was no sign of life. It felt like a bad dream. At this point we knew one person had died and more than 70 homes had been destroyed, along with hundreds of sheds and vehicles. I felt guilty that my house was still standing.

Driving the winding roads of the Adelaide Hills, the scorched scenery felt endless. Blackened tree stumps lined the edge of roads and covered the hillsides. Some trees still had their leaves, but they were curled, orange and petrified; they had suffered in the heat. The black trees were the lucky ones; others were reduced to mounds of ash.

I was on my way to meet Mount Torrens residents Ray and Barbara Offe. I had heard they were among the few people in the area who had chosen to stay and defend. They were not expecting us.

My cameraman Trent Murphy and I pulled into their long, steep, winding, driveway and it took a few minutes before their mudbrick house came into sight. It was intact, sitting pretty at the top of the highest point in sight. The fire had crept right up to their front and back doors, leaving a black perimeter around the house. From their front porch I could see all the way out to the surrounding townships. A bird's-eye view of the hills, it was spectacular, but for all the wrong reasons.

A sceptical Ray Offe greeted Trent and me through his screen door at the side of his house. He was shocked we wanted to talk to him and hear his story, but I guess it is not every day you open your front door to see a reporter on your porch. Their property stretches for acres, far from any neighbours and in the middle of dense scrub and trees. 'It was all thanks to these,' he said, pointing to the sprinkler heads installed on his roof. 'They saved our house. It's the reason it's still standing.'

The couple were yet to get their power back on and were running a generator to get water to their house. They seemed exhausted but happy to share their story. Their biggest relief was they were safe and the house they had built in 1990 had survived.

Ray shut the screen door and led us from under his carport on the righthand side of the house, down a small paved path to a green iron shed, built into the side of a hill. The shed door squealed as he slid it open, the rollers fighting against the layers of ash in the tracks. The shed was big enough to comfortably house a motorhome and a car.

Mount Torrens residents Ray and Barbara Offe. (Brittany Evins)

Geoff Weaver cleaning up his burnt-out shed, Lenswood, SA. (Brittany Evins)

'This is it, this is where we were,' Ray pointed to the back of the shed, to a solid metal door partially hidden behind the motorhome. The door looked to be a standard size, big enough to walk through without bending down, nestled into a grey slab of concrete.

'Yeah, right back there, that's our bunker. We built it ourselves, but the Cudlee Creek fire was the first time we got to trial it – thankfully it worked well. It was very, very noisy, hot, smoky and a little bit scary. You just have to lie on the ground with a blanket over you,' he explained. 'The doors are really tight-fitting. We've got water down there, we've got breathing masks.'

I did not get to see inside the bunker; it was too soon for Ray to step back inside.

Ray and Barbara had spent more than an hour in their bunker braving the fire front, and I could tell it was tough recounting the experience.

Barbara had stepped away and was dropping some seed onto the ashy soil for the resident kangaroos. 'This is Cheeky and that one there is Mrs Slow,' Barbara said, gesturing to the kangaroos in front of us before walking a few steps towards a concrete water trough and turning the tap on. The kangaroos were close enough that you could reach out and touch them. Barbara and Ray had picked up some extra food for them from a donation site at a town nearby.

—

Kangaroos were becoming a regular feature of Adelaide Hills residents' stories of survival. In Lenswood, about ten minutes down the road from Barbara and Ray, wine producer Geoff Weaver was cleaning up sheets of iron. They were the remnants of his shed. Looking at what was left, it was hard to picture it standing tall just days ago. The only tell-tale signs it had been a shed were the warped sheets of iron and the shattered wine bottles below them – bottles kept from sentimental vintages, Geoff told us. Molten aluminium fingers ran down the hill from under his burnt-out car.

Geoff had lost his former house, built on the same property, in the 1983 Ash Wednesday fires. He described the pain that the loss had caused him and his family, believing that if he had been there that Wednesday in 1983, he could have defended his home. After that day, Geoff had vowed to stay and defend, a promise he now regretted.

He spoke of how rapidly the recent fire had spread to his property. Watching the plume of smoke in the distance, at least three towns away, he thought he would be safe. Then the wall of fire was in his trees and the whole of the eastern hill of his property was alight.

We drove for a few minutes from the top of his property, where his shed and burnt-out car were, down past rows of vineyards. We pulled up on a small clearing and walked a few metres down to his dam. 'If I didn't make it to this dam, I don't think I'd be here today,' Geoff explained. 'This is where

I was sitting. I was sharing it with a kangaroo and watching the flames and hearing the explosions.' Geoff and the kangaroo sat on opposite sides of the dam for what seemed like hours, keeping each other company.

The first explosions he had heard were from gas bottles and belongings in the small stone cabin that he had re-built after 1983. Then an explosion and a plume of black smoke came from the shed, as the fire consumed his car, which was parked inside.

From the dam, he could feel the scorching heat of the flames, but was thankful for the fresh water and for the firebreak provided by the green grass surrounding him.

The Cudlee Creek fire destroyed 30 per cent of his vineyard and engulfed his shed, car and cabin. He counts himself as one of the lucky ones, though, and is thankful he still has 70 per cent of his vineyard, allowing him to maintain income into the future.

—

It was about three weeks since I had met Barbara and Ray Offe at their Mount Torrens home. In the meantime, I had been sent to Kangaroo Island to report on the bushfire emergency there. The impact was incomprehensible. The fires had ripped through the island, killing two people and burning around half the island.

It was about 4 o'clock in the afternoon and I was sitting on the floor of my hotel room on Kangaroo Island, preparing for a live cross to the afternoon television news, when my phone rang.

It was Ray Offe. He told me about the strong winds that had been blowing ash into their house and how the naked trees were exposing them to sounds of nature they had never heard before. He updated me on the kangaroos still taking refuge at their home. The two mother roos and their youngsters were healthy and had warmed to pats. Other stragglers and displaced roos would pass by from time to time, darting through the blackened hillside. He told me he could see a young koala grazing in a tree.

When I asked about Barbara he paused, sighed and told me she had been diagnosed with cancer. She was set to have two surgeries and was still considering chemotherapy. Radiotherapy and hormone therapy would take place in a week or two.

'Fingers crossed, but we feel she has dodged a bullet at this point in time, as her surgeon was very upbeat with progress,' Ray said. 'However, cancer is just one of those crappy diseases that can crop up again or simply hide elsewhere so easily and, even with all the chemo, can still prevail.'

He was surprisingly optimistic and told me of their donations over the years to cancer organisations, never thinking they would be the ones going through it.

Over the previous month, I had seen so much devastation, pain and suffering in the communities I had been reporting on, and even though I had done what I could on the ground through my job and had donated to a few local fundraising initiatives, I felt I needed to do more. The connection I had built with so many of these incredibly strong, brave and resilient people compelled me to go one step further.

After hearing about Barbara Offe's cancer diagnosis, I decided to make my own contribution by cutting off my hair and raising money for a cancer organisation. It took me a few weeks to build up the courage because, for me, this was a big decision. After 25 years of living with long hair, which I had never cut, I thought my hair was my identity.

Despite not being directly related to the bushfires, this was something I could contribute, something that might one day help someone like Barbara who had been dealt such a terrible hand.

In the end, cutting my hair was easy. What challenged me this summer was merely doing my job. Reporting on an active fire ground and telling the stories of the people who were impacted days, weeks and even months later is hard, but it is so important for our community. I feel thankful I had the opportunity to inform the thousands of people at risk, and to see the faces of people who had been almost broken by the flames but who are now on their own journey to recovery.

Brittany Evins is a journalist for Adelaide's ABC News

One, Two, Three, Breathe

Adriane Reardon

It's quite a sight looking out your back door and seeing burnt leaves fall from the sky. You do a double-take because you're unsure at first what they are. They could be bugs or moths flying about at dusk. Maybe the sunset is playing tricks on your eyes. You go outside, look up and see them twirling in the sky. Big leaves, little ones, partially burnt leaves, even some burnt tree bark. They spiral down in the breeze, fast and frantic in their turns before they land at your feet. They were once soft green eucalyptus leaves, the same ones you can fold to inhale a sweet perfume. But these ones aren't soft. They are brittle. They keep falling. You start gathering them in your hands where they leave black stains and they crumble under your toes when you walk.

It was 30 December 2019 when this happened to me. The burnt leaves came. They came some more. And then they eased. I still see them every now and them, blown into a bush, caught between the rocks or washed up on the beach. Now they don't faze me so much. I've become used to the sight of them. When I pick them up I actually breathe a sigh of relief, because a burnt leaf is one thing, but at least it's not hot.

The far south coast of New South Wales is my home. It's a quiet nook and beautifully defined by its diverse landscape. It's only two and a half hours' drive from the sea to the snow, with the parts in between filled with small towns and localities – many of which are difficult to pronounce without guidance from the locals. Farming in the region is dominated by dairy, cattle and seafood, and prominent industries include tourism, health and local government. There are strong creative talents in art and music but also sport and athletics. The region is made up of three local government areas: the Bega Valley, Eurobodalla and Snowy Monaro shires. By late 2019 the drought had sucked the ground dry. And then the bushfires started. Nearly a thousand homes, as well as sheds, livestock and fencing, were destroyed across the three shires during the 2019–20 bushfire season.

There were hundreds of people who helped fight those fires, some together and some alone. Many of them had prior experience battling a fire, but for others it would be their first time. The courage displayed by those on the fire ground was inspirational, none more so than that shown by John Gallagher and Nathan Barden.

They had never worked together until New Year's Eve 2019. Nathan was 26 and John 34 when the two teamed up in Quaama, a small village in the Bega Valley in between Cobargo and Bega. They each had 11 years' experience volunteering for the New South Wales RFS. Both were calm and cool-headed in emergency situations. Fire, in most forms, didn't bother them because they knew it could be controlled.

Despite the warnings, John and Nathan expected the summer of 2019–20 to be like any other fire season they had seen over the past decade. It had been a dry year and they were prepared for a handful of nasty, hot days. They expected signature strong winds to fan flames that might be started by lightning strikes or a spark from a campfire or welder. Some fires would be more challenging than others, but the firies would eventually put them out. They always go out. But as it transpired, this season wasn't like any other. John and Nathan would be caught off guard by the fear, tragedy, destruction and ultimately death that the bushfires would bring. The fires would burn hot into their memories, and visions of that day would continue to haunt them.

—

Nathan Barden had been called out to fight his first fire as a volunteer with the RFS in December 2009. He was 16 years old at the time. His father, Clem Barnden, was also a devoted volunteer with the Jellat fire brigade in the Bega Valley shire. Growing up, whenever his dad was sent out on a job, Nathan would wait anxiously for him to come home, ready with questions about how it all went down. Nathan was 15 years old when he watched coverage of the 2009 Black Saturday fires on the television. He had never seen fires so horrific. He wanted to help fight it. He wasn't afraid. In October of that same year, he signed up to the RFS.

Ten years later, Nathan was fighting the worst bushfires the country had seen. He was as courageous at 26 as he had been at 16. His drive to help others in need had never failed him in the decade that he'd already served, but he had never before seen fires like these ones. He not only feared for the lives of others, he also feared for his own. For the first time tackling a bushfire, Nathan was afraid.

> 'When you hear someone's life is in immediate danger, you can't not try. But I was afraid. There wasn't a single fire front: everything was on fire.' – Nathan Barnden

On 30 December 2019, Nathan was working in Canberra, a three-hour drive away from Bega. The Werri Berri bushfire near Bemboka, northwest of Bega, was escalating and Nathan left work to help defend his home ground; if it came to it, he'd be there. He also needed to return to the Bega Valley to visit his grandmother. Her health was failing and the family was preparing to say their goodbyes at her nursing home. But Nathan didn't want to think about that now. He just needed to get to Bemboka to fight this damn fire.

The drive from Canberra to Bega's fire control centre passed quickly. When he arrived in Bega, he was assigned the role of strike team leader, in charge of coordinating firefighting resources. He hopped into an RFS car and made his way to Bemboka. He saw fires ahead of the Werri Berri bushfire spotting into properties near the intersection of Buckajo Road and the Snowy Mountains Highway. Nathan's task was to prevent the fire from jumping the highway. He worked throughout the evening with five or so crews putting out spot fires and containing the blaze to one side of the road. By 11 pm, the situation had calmed and many volunteers headed home to rest. Nathan stayed back with three other trucks and their crews to see the night through.

Then midnight came and, like clockwork, everything changed. Nathan received reports of triple-zero calls coming from Upper Brogo Road at Quaama, northeast of Bemboka. The Badja Forest Road fire was making its way through the remote mountainside, heading east. Surely it would take at least another day for it to threaten any towns? There was no way the fire could move that fast.

> 'I've never been more wrong in my life.' – Nathan Barnden

Nathan escorted his remaining crew members to Quaama to understand how threatening the fire front actually was. He saw three fires spot ahead of the main fire front. It was certainly picking up. He and his crews attempted to fight the blazes out, but the front chewed through the hillside with anger and ease. Within an hour, there were 20 spot fires. And then 30. Then 40. It was not slowing down. Nathan could feel the intense heat radiating from the hills; the smoke in the air had thickened. As dawn approached, Nathan pulled his crew back to Quaama. They were no longer playing offence. It was time to defend.

Moments before 5 am on New Year's Eve, Nathan was moved into the role of divisional commander. He went from coordinating five trucks to coordinating more than a dozen, and began overseeing tactics and strategies to defend the locality of Quaama.

Two kilometres north of the Quaama fire station was Nardy House, a property that provides accommodation and respite to people with physical disabilities. A fire was moving in erratic directions and was difficult to track, but it posed a threat to the accommodation. Nathan decided to start charging its way. Unless Nardy House was defended, it would be one of the first properties in Quaama to be burnt.

Fortunately, all of the occupants had been evacuated. When Nathan got to Nardy House, he assigned three trucks to stay and defend the building. One of the volunteer firefighters there was his father, Clem, working under Nathan's command. The fire front was burning about 500 metres away in a paddock, making its way through grassland with flames stretching four to five metres high. There wasn't much fuel on the ground, though, so crews expected the fire would die down by the time it reached the fringe of the Nardy House property. With the situation thought to be under control, Nathan said goodbye to his father and the crew and walked back to his car, to monitor the situation elsewhere. And just then, as he opened his car door, like striking a match, the place was ablaze.

> 'Before I could shut the car door, everything exploded. The fire went from being 500 metres away to on top of the crews. It was so loud that I couldn't hear the radio in the vehicle I was sitting in. I had no defensive gear on me so I pulled my door shut to protect my body from the heat. I looked in the rear-view-vision mirror and the last thing I saw was Dad and the entire crew disappear in fire.' – Nathan Barnden

Flames roared 40 metres high and gum trees exploded from the heat, encircling Nardy House in fire. The blaze encompassed the entire crew in light, heat and smoke. If Nathan were to have stepped outside the shelter of his vehicle, he would have been burnt alive. One minute passed. The fire continued to burn bright. Two minutes passed. And then the fire began to move away. The front passed as quickly as it came, moving south towards the main Quaama township.

There are three colours used by the RFS to communicate over radio the severity of a situation. The first is yellow, which represents a general non-incident-related call. The second colour is blue, which is used to indicate an operational incident-related call. Then there is red, which means urgent assistance is needed because the lives of others are under threat. For the first time in Nathan's career as a firefighter, he yelled red into the vehicle's two-way radio.

He didn't know it then, but he would use it another 25 times as the hours went on. After relaying the message through the truck radio, he found himself running. As fast as he could. He was looking for someone, anyone, who was alive. Nearby trees were ablaze and the walls of Nardy House were scorched. But where was the crew? Where was his dad? In the haze, he spotted the volunteers on their backs, hoses armed above their chests. The force of the fire had thrown them to the ground and the heat had turned the water from their hoses into steam. It was a miracle they were alive. He kept running and found a second crew alive. And then the third. And then he found his dad. He hugged him tight and they both cried into each other's collars. But the fire was still moving towards Quaama. So, pulling himself together, Nathan once again farewelled his father, ran back to his vehicle and drove on.

Nathan had to work quickly. Speaking through the car's radio, he instructed crews at the Quaama fire station to move all of the residents to one location and to prepare to defend the site. Fire trucks and other RFS vehicles had been set up to circle the station, a defensive line to protect those inside. As soon as Nathan arrived at the fire station, the blaze arrived. It burnt as furiously as it had at Nardy House. And then it moved quickly, south and east, chewing through properties across town. Triple-zero calls were coming in thick and fast with reports of people trapped in their homes. Nathan knew he needed to help. But he couldn't do it alone. He needed a partner.

That's when he met John Gallagher.

—

On Monday, 30 December, John Gallagher was with his family enjoying a ritual lunch on the back deck of his home in Tathra. As a force of habit, he had the two-way radio on in the background. It was always handy listening in, as he had learnt on 18 March 2018 when a bushfire impacted parts of Tarraganda, Reedy Swamp and Tathra, all east of Bega. The area had lost 65 homes and 35 cabins and caravans that day. Almost two years on and the memories were still fresh.

As well as being a volunteer for the RFS, John also used to be a paramedic, so the habit of tuning into emergency communications had never left him. As he turned the sausages

Adriane Reardon reporting from Bega evacuation centre. (Daniel Doody/ABC)

A ute destroyed by fire in the NSW town of Quaama. (Matt Roberts/ABC)

and the chicken skewers, he overheard reports of fire activity increasing in Bemboka, nearly 40 kilometres west of Bega and about 45 minutes' drive from Tathra.

The day so far had been benign. But as soon as he was ready to bring out the salads and bread, the radio chatter increased and smoke started drifting over the sky. John knew something wasn't right. He dropped the tongs and said a quick goodbye to his family, who were familiar with him going off to fight a fire at the drop of a hat. He headed to his local brigade where he hastily changed into his yellow RFS uniform and made his way out to Bemboka along with his brigade captain, Adam Wiggins.

John had known this day was coming. Fires had been burning up and down New South Wales for months and he had a gut feeling they would eventually make their way to the Bega Valley. Today was that day.

> 'It was inevitable that it would roll into the Bega Valley. We couldn't escape it. But what I didn't know was how long it would keep going for. It really just didn't give up.' – John Gallagher

At a farm in Bemboka, John worked alongside more than a dozen firefighters late into the evening putting out hotspots that had been jumping out from the Werri Berri bushfire. The fire was steadily making its way through the nearby mountain range, and volunteers and farmers were working together to prepare the properties that would come under threat if it trickled its way down the hillside. John had fought fires like this before and, by 11 pm, the bushfire was still a reasonable distance away so they decided to head home while another crew stayed to defend the property until dawn. Approaching his car, he met a man by the name of Patrick Salway who had come to lend a hand.

> 'I stopped and had a chat with Patrick. We chewed the fat a little bit, had a laugh and went on our way. I was expecting to go home after that. I thought it was done and dusted.' – John Gallagher

It was now midnight. John and Adam hopped into their truck and within the 20 minutes it took them to drive east from Bemboka along the Snowy Mountains Highway to the intersection with the Princes Highway, the situation changed dramatically. The pair were getting calls about fires popping up in Brogo, about 30 minutes north of Bega, so instead of heading home to Tathra, they headed north and proceeded to McLeod Hill. There they met up with teams of other firefighters who had located a spot fire that was spreading fast to a neighbouring property. These flames weren't spotting from the Werri Berri bushfire. They were coming from an entirely separate front: the Badja Forest Road fire, which was also burning its way southeast. John worked alongside the other volunteers and police to evacuate the area and to put out this new fire. But it was a stubborn one and it jumped the highway, eventually burning into Mumbulla Mountain.

> 'It really started to ramp up. We thought we were dealing with bread-and-butter spot fires. When we realised it had got into the mountain range, we were facing a completely different beast.' – John Gallagher

Radio traffic suddenly became busy with more calls for help within Quaama, a five-minute drive north on the Princes Highway, which was being threatened by this new fire. By 2 am, John was driving along Verona Road, west of Quaama, to try to locate its front. Five kilometres from the township, he spotted it. Based on the location, he knew houses would already have been lost, but he was hopeful they could still save Quaama. Hot temperatures and strong winds fuel and fan bushfires, but in Quaama there was little to no wind at the time, and being the middle of the night, still somewhat cool. Conditions are on our side for now, thought John. He could see the fire was only gradually making its way through remote country and into open paddocks. It wouldn't be able to reach the township at this pace. Surely not.

But by 3 am the temperature had risen to 34 degrees. The humidity was low and the wind had picked up significantly. Back in the town of Quaama, John watched the growing and glowing fire in the mountain range from a lookout. It wasn't looking good.

By 4 am, John started to hear the first sign of trouble along Verona Road, the same road he had driven on just hours earlier. Reports were coming in of people unable to defend their properties and retreating to Quaama. Taking another drive to the fire front John spotted the blaze only two kilometres out of town. It was heading straight for Quaama. And nothing was going to stop it. Embers started flying overhead in the hot wind, which pushed through the trees and streets lining the township. Residents started running to the local fire shed for shelter and dozens of firefighters stood outside it preparing for the battle ahead.

At 5.30 am on New Year's Eve, the fire hit Quaama with a ruthless ferocity. At this hour, it should have been sunrise, but smoke had masked the sky, casting a deep-red hue across town. The Quaama fire station was filled with about 30 people, including children, now all donning face masks. John, alongside the other firefighters, tried to reassure them but could see the terror in their eyes. The dozen firefighters there made the decision that they were not equipped to defend the whole town with the few resources they had. But they could defend the fire station and the people in it.

A gust of wind brought flames onto the fire station's doorstep. John ran outside, his eyes stinging from the heat. Trees caught alight, gas bottles outside exploded and the power went out.

Only the red and blue lights from the eight or so fire trucks continued to flash in the chaos. Squinting, John managed to find the pump on his fire truck and rolled out a hose, aiming it at a wall of fire. The flames laughed at him and blew the water back in his face. He held his ground trying his best to subdue the blaze. Then he was running to find more water among the spaghetti of fire hoses because the tank connected to his truck had run dry, then sprinting back. How long was he fighting the flames around the station? Ten minutes? Twenty? The fire began to move past the shed and across the road and so the crews moved with it. A house caught fire. Others down the street were ablaze. But the main front had passed through Quaama.

—

John Gallagher knew of Nathan Barnden, but they had not yet officially met. It was the country, after all; everybody had heard of everybody. Tathra RFS captain Adam Wiggins helped pair them together at the Quaama fire station, but it wasn't the time for an elaborate introduction. Both wanting to help, they decided to get moving. John's vehicle was assigned to other firefighters, so they found themselves in the same standard SUV Nathan had been driving all night. It wasn't ideal. The car was built for transport, not for putting out fires. There were no defensive hoses, no internal curtain on the windscreen to protect them from the heat of the glass. But it had a radio and fuel. And that was enough. Nathan took the wheel, and John coordinated radio communications in the passenger seat. Although both had been responding to fires since yesterday afternoon, the days felt like they were rolling into one.

Their first stop was a property on Whitby Wilsons Road, just north of Quaama, where five children and two adults were reportedly trapped inside their burning house. The road to the property was a treacherous one. The Princes Highway was melting from the heat. The headlights on the vehicle were on high beam, straining to light a path through the thick smoke. Trees on the side of the road were falling at random and Nathan managed to dodge those that had rolled onto the road. Nearing the property, they turned onto a winding road surrounded by dense forest, completely ablaze. Even inside the car, their eyes were stinging.

They arrived at the property to see three-quarters of the house engulfed in flames along with parts of the veranda. The family's car was on fire. No one was outside defending the house. No one could be seen. Nathan stayed in the car and kept the motor running as John ran towards the house. He yanked open the back door to find a family of seven on the lounge room floor, huddled under blankets, counting to three and breathing into paper bags. The kids were not wearing any shoes or shirts. The family was scared and had been caught completely unaware by the inferno. *One, two, three.*

The wooden stairs of the veranda suddenly caught fire, so the adults passed the kids to John over the balcony railing. Once they made it to the ground, the children ran barefoot over embers and debris to Nathan's car. Once all nine were squeezed in, they began their journey back to Quaama. Embers and twigs rained on the vehicle as they sped through the burning forest back to the highway. 'Are we going to die?' asked one of the children. John and Nathan didn't know what to say. Both thought they just might.

The heat was unrelenting and John and Nathan told the kids to crouch low in the back seat away from the hot glass in case it shattered. Along narrow roads and through multiple fire fronts, they made it back to the Quaama fire station, the car's temperature gauge off the charts and the check-engine light aglow. But the family was safe.

—

Triple-zero calls on the car's radio kept coming, so John and Nathan left the family at Quaama and headed out to another rescue, this time to reports of a property with an elderly couple inside. They headed back up the Princes Highway, again through walls of fire and past falling trees. John directed Nathan to take a right onto Christophers Road. The street was completely alight. Mailboxes and fence posts were burning. Metal fences were melting and trees were falling. John and

Nathan were 200 metres from where they needed to get to but the road before them was impenetrable. A wall of fire stood between them and the house.

> 'The car was rocking and being hammered by debris. There was fire everywhere and you can't see anything. John and I made a decision that we couldn't physically go any further – and if we did, we would die. How far do you push your own life to save someone else?' – Nathan Barnden

Nathan turned the SUV around and drove back to the highway, while John called for additional trucks and firefighters to help them get through. While waiting for back-up to arrive, they opened the car's bonnet and every door to cool the vehicle down. They tried not to think about what was going on behind that wall of fire, whether the couple were being burnt alive. They couldn't leave them. They wouldn't.

By the time their car had cooled and the check-engine light had switched off, fire trucks had arrived. With both dread and determination, John and Nathan headed back down Christophers Road. This time, they drove behind the force of sturdy fire trucks, which managed to make a safe-enough break through the wall of fire to allow access to the house. They found the couple defending their home. The ravenous fire front had already passed by the property so John and Nathan provided brief assistance to the pair and handed them masks before moving on to the next call.

They didn't have to drive far this time. A woman was reportedly trapped at her property just down the street. By now, the road was riddled with fallen trees, so John and Nathan drove over a nature strip to get to the house. When they arrived, they found a badly burnt woman injured in her driveway. Clothes singed, eyelashes melted. She was still breathing, though struggling. Arm in arm, John walked the woman to the vehicle and rushed her back to the Quaama fire shed in the hope a paramedic would come to her aid. She was alive. But barely. There were reports the highway had become too hazardous for paramedics to get through so, in a risky move, Tathra brigade captain Adam Wiggins rushed the woman to the hospital in Bega, navigating burning logs and debris.

—

Three rescues together for these two strangers in the most horrific and devastating scenarios each had ever seen in their combined 22-year history volunteering for the RFS. The day was not over for either of them, but their partnership was. John continued to fight fires and defend homes between Quaama and Cobargo for the rest of the day.

Nathan stayed in Quaama to coordinate resources. But his life was about to change forever.

It was about 8 am on New Year's Eve. Nathan was sitting in the driver's seat of the SUV, parked near the Quaama fire station. Quaama was still on fire and he was using the vehicle's radio to try to get more firefighters in.

Someone tapped on his window. He recognised the man as a member of his Jellat brigade. Nathan ignored him; he was busy and didn't have time to talk. The man tapped again and said that Nathan needed to come with him. He got out of the vehicle. The man led him to Clem, Nathan's dad, who looked very upset. His eyes were red, watery.

> 'Dad's not the kind to cry. I've never seen him do it. I thought Nanna must have passed away. She was on her deathbed. That must have been what happened. I walked down to Dad and he just looked me in the face and said, "Patrick and Robert are dead."' – Nathan Barnden

Nathan learnt then that his uncle Robert Salway and his cousin Patrick had died while defending their property in Wandella. His aunty had found their bodies.

> 'You know when you watch movies and you always think someone's exaggerating when they find out something horrific and their legs give out from under them? I always thought that was something stupid they did in cinema. Until it happened to me. I remember kneeling

there in the middle of the road. Just bawling my eyes out whilst Quaama burnt around me.' – Nathan Barnden

Nathan's younger brother, Michael, was also there helping to fight the fires in the town. The brothers and their dad mourned together. They embraced and shed tears. They only had minutes. Then Nathan, Michael and Clem walked past the evacuees into the back room of the Quaama fire station where they found a phone. Together, they called Nathan and Michael's mother, Rosey, who did not yet know the news. As Rosey sat by her mother's side, she learnt that her brother and nephew had died.

It was a cruel blow, but Nathan decided he had to keep going. His sense of duty unwavering, he continued to fight fires between Cobargo, Quaama and Brogo for another six hours until he was told by his crew members to leave. It was time for him to go home and rest. In a convoy of about 30 cars, Nathan led residents of Quaama along the highway littered with burning tree limbs to Bega's evacuation centre, with his father and brother in tow. Then he went to the nursing home to see his mother and grandmother, where they mourned as a family. His grandmother, Edna Salway, would pass away the next day.

—

Nathan and John continued to fight fires across the Bega Valley in the coming weeks, assisting crews across the region. Nathan hasn't slept well since the night of New Year's Eve 2019, and John continues to reflect on the horror of it. Nathan and John have since reunited with a lot of the people they met that day, including the family of seven who had been huddled in their living room counting to three. When Nathan and John went back to the property together weeks later, they found that the home had burnt completely to the ground.

> 'It was quite a confronting moment to stand there in front of that property in the weeks later and to look at where they were. To think that there would be seven bodies that were inside that home. But there aren't. And that's all we can be thankful for.' – Nathan Barnden

Adriane Reardon is a reporter at ABC South East NSW based in Bega

Currowan on the Run

Jessie Davies

A MAILBOX. THAT'S ALL THAT WAYNE DUNCAN RECOGNISED when he returned to his Conjola Park home on 1 January. Tall and red, it had once stood under a shady tree. Now, like everything nearby, it was shrivelled and blackened.

'I don't even have the key,' Wayne said as he kicked around in the ashes of his home.

His beloved weekender – a two-bedroom place with panoramic views of Lake Conjola – was gone. The day before, Wayne had fled as the deathly Currowan bushfire bore down on the fishing village on the New South Wales south coast.

The fire had been burning to the west of the Princes Highway, and RFS crews had worked backburning bushland near Yatte Yattah, just inland from Lake Conjola, to protect properties in the area. It remains unclear if the main fire or the backburn spotted across the containment line, but fierce winds whipped up and pushed the fire towards the coast.

At 10.28 am on New Year's Eve the RFS sent an emergency mobile alert, warning more than 2000 people in the Conjola area to 'seek shelter as the fire arrives'. But many residents across Conjola and Yatte Yattah received no official warnings that day.

Wayne had stayed to defend his home. For hours he attacked embers with wet towels, but as the fire's rumble grew louder and the sun disappeared, Wayne knew it was time to go.

'It just got so black we couldn't see. It was intense,' he said. He sought shelter in a friend's home, closer to the lake's edge. 'All we could hear were loud explosions. We just sat and waited.'

Residents called for the help of the RFS, but crews couldn't immediately respond. Fire had claimed key access roads in the area, which made it difficult for trucks to pass.

Later, ABC reporters Sean Rubinsztein-Dunlop and John Stewart would interview firefighter John Moore, who was part of a team of 17 urban firefighters who braced the flames to drive their trucks into Conjola Park. 'The behaviour of that fire was something I haven't seen in 36 years of attending bushfires,' John Moore told them. 'We saw gas balls in the air, and they were igniting 30 to 40 metres in the air – I've never seen anything like that before.'

Water-bombing aircraft retreated because of high winds. John called for help many times. 'I did require assistance on that day but there was no timely assistance available due to the nature of the fires on the south coast,' he said.

Three people in the Lake Conjola district lost their lives as the fire passed through. Laurie Andrew, 70, died outside his home at Yatte Yattah, while John Butler, 75, was found dead in a burnt-out car near the Princes Highway in the same locality. Michael Campbell, aged 62, was found dead in a vehicle in Sussex Inlet.

Eighty-nine properties were burnt to the ground. As water pressure in the area plummeted, some residents tried to douse the flames with beer, milk and steaks.

Seeing the damage for myself on 2 January was astonishing. Driving into the small idyllic inlet just 18 kilometres north of Ulladulla, I couldn't believe my eyes. I saw cars with aluminium features that had melted into a puddle. I saw exposed bedrooms, their walls and roofs ripped off and their steel bed frames laid bare. Charred trucks; razed boats and caravans.

Over my reporting career I had covered bushfires before, but none on this scale. The heartbreak was palpable. But among the rubble there were stories of hope, heart and heroism. While trying to find mobile reception atop a hill that day, my colleague Kelly Fuller and I encountered Yama Khatiz. He invited us to his home to tell us his story.

At about 11 am on New Year's Eve, Yama told us, he and his family were about to go for a swim when they noticed a water-

Jessie Davies interviewing Yama Khatiz in Lake Conjola, NSW. (Kelly Fuller/ABC)

Camera operator Luke Stephenson films a cottage destroyed by the Currowan fire at Pebbly Beach. (Tom Lowrey/ABC)

bombing helicopter filling up from the lake. Then, without warning, flames engulfed their street.

'We thought about leaving, but at that moment our neighbour's roof caught on fire and spot fires started all around us,' Yama said. 'There was nowhere to go.'

Yama, along with his father, Zalmai, his mum, Kathy, his wife, Karen, and their four teenage children didn't hesitate. 'Everybody got a bucket of water and was running everywhere,' Zalmai said. 'One moment the children's playground [on the lake's shore nearby] was on fire and we were pouring water on it. Then our other neighbour's house caught on fire, so we ran over there.'

With buckets of water filled from garden taps, the family managed to not only save their own house but also the houses of elderly neighbours who needed help.

Zalmai said he felt a sense of duty to give back to the community that had welcomed him nearly 40 years ago, after he had migrated to Australia from Afghanistan. 'Australia gave us a future,' he said. 'Now, I feel like we are in debt to give to other Australians.'

—

A week earlier, Christmas had been tense for south Nowra farmer John Bennett.

His cattle property was threatened by the Comberton bushfire on 22 December, when repeated ember attacks sparked grass fires nearby. John spent his Christmas break patrolling. Many sleepless nights later, the Comberton bushfire was downgraded to 'watch and act'.

But as New Year's Eve inched closer, so too did another fire. It was the deadly Currowan blaze. Fuelled by low humidity and tinder-dry vegetation, the fire marched northward, straight towards Nowra, home to more than 30,000 people.

By 3 January, John's farm was one of the last parcels of land standing between the fire and the southern edge of the city. John felt a desperate sense of duty to protect his land. He established containment lines around his property, using heavy machinery to clear away flammable vegetation, and began patrolling with a mobile firefighting unit. But his task was never going to be easy. The reason? John's farm was filled with peat moss – a highly flammable substance that can burn deep underground for metres, even in damp conditions.

'If fire got into our place, which is also filled with swamp grass, it would be impossible to put out,' he said.

That week, while John and his father, Merv, sat sentry on their boundary fence, they watched dozens of snakes slither out from their swampy home and slither toward the township of Nowra.

'Mother Nature knows what's happening and they're getting out of here,' John said.

Two of his dogs suffered snake bites. Thankfully, he said, that was the worst of it.

On 4 January, the fire shifted direction and tore through the Nowra Hill area, to the west of the Princes Highway. John's farm had been spared. But as the blaze took a dangerous run north, the day's trouble was only just beginning for residents in Kangaroo Valley.

—

'Billy goat country.' That's how Kangaroo Valley RFS divisional commander Andrew Fielding described the terrain between the Shoalhaven River at North Nowra and Kangaroo Valley.

For weeks, Andrew had known the Currowan fire was coming. Prolonged drought had dried up the Shoalhaven River and, in many stretches, vegetation reached from one side to the other, providing a clear run for any fire. Once over the river, it could surge unimpeded for thousands of square kilometres.

Andrew's crews helped throughout the Shoalhaven area in the weeks leading up to New Year's Eve, but rested when they could, all the while keeping close to the valley. Waiting. Watching. Listening for news that the fire had spotted over the river. 'We knew the river wouldn't stop it. There was no chance,' Andrew said.

A brief moment of hope ensued as firefighters fought the blaze in the wider Nowra area, but at 6 pm on 4 January the news came: the fire had reached Tallowa Dam, located on the northern side of Shoalhaven River, downstream from the river's confluence with the Kangaroo River. From there, it had started to sprint through deep gullies and into the Morton National Park. It was heading straight towards Kangaroo Valley, home to almost 1000 people.

'On that day the temperature was high, the humidity was low and there was a lot of ground cover that could burn. It was the perfect recipe,' Andrew said.

As night fell, the gusty conditions, dry landscape and sheer size of the fire created an overwhelming sense of dread. Fanned by winds of 90 kilometres an hour, the fire spread rapidly. It created its own weather system and ran straight over the bush community of Budgong and took out multiple houses in the west of Kangaroo Valley along Tallowa Dam Road, Mount Scanzi Road and Jacks Corner Road.

The strong southerly wind meant the eastern townships of North Nowra and Cambewarra escaped the blaze. Thousands of people there had been evacuated, and all returned home after the fire marched northward.

The same could not be said for Kangaroo Valley. Wolter Peeters, a photographer with the *Sydney Morning Herald*, arrived in the valley early on Sunday, 5 January, and captured the destruction. Driving along Tallowa Dam Road, the devastation wrought by the Currowan blaze was clear to see. Trees in excess of 30 metres had been stripped bare. Houses were reduced to sheets of flat iron. Powerlines lay flat, their wires in mangled messes on the forest floor. Wombats roamed aimlessly.

'As my colleague and I were driving, all conversation ceased,' Wolter said. 'We just thought, wow, this is intense.'

Wolter came across a burnt-out four-wheel drive and, later, its owner. The man identified himself as a National Parks and Wildlife Services employee and told Wolter that his vehicle had been immobilised at the height of the fire when it hit a fallen tree. He and a colleague had escaped the firestorm and sought refuge in a dam for three hours.

'They had cut through a wire fence [and] scrambled up an embankment to safety,' Wolter said. More than five houses had been lost in Kangaroo Valley, but Alexander Michael's home escaped untouched. Walking onto his property, my colleague Caitlin Dugan and I jumped fallen power lines and trees still smouldering from the horror of the previous night.

Fire had scorched the five-acre block, but Alexander's house was in immaculate condition and shone bright like a beacon. A black barn-style build, the industrial-inspired structure featured yellow shipping containers on the second floor. His lights were on, his water running. His lawn was green.

Alexander, a Sydney-based industrial designer, had constructed the house and crafted the garden to withstand severe fire conditions. 'I went a little bit overboard – and now I'm thanking Christ I did,' he said. His home was built with five-millimetre-thick plate steel and six-millimetre-thick toughened glass. All the gutters had ember proofing on them and there was no plastic used on the exterior finishes. 'The fact it's still standing is testament to how well it was built.'

—

The carnage continued beyond Kangaroo Valley into the Southern Highlands. At 10 pm on 4 January, David Stimson's family were sitting around the kitchen table in their Wingello home.

David stared out the window into the darkness. He could see the glow of the fire and knew it was burning unusually fast. He turned and said to his son, 'I think the train is coming.'

'We could hear the roar of the fire. LPG gas bottles were exploding. Glass was shattering,' David said later.

Meanwhile, in nearby Bundanoon, Donna Andrews and John Grono had trouble on their hands. Earlier, a massive pyrocumulonimbus cloud sitting above the Morton National Park had collapsed, causing a monstrous downdraft of wind that barrelled the Currowan mega-fire towards the Southern Highlands, starting the Morton fire.

Totally unaware the fire had started down the road, Donna and John received a panicked phone call from a neighbour: 'We're on fire, get out, get out, get out!'

Donna and John still couldn't see any flames on their Yuille Avenue property. But they fled. As their cars merged onto

Jake Lapham photographs the aftermath of the Currowan fire along Braidwood Road. (Sarah Moss/ABC)

Bundanoon Road, they were faced with flames on both sides of the road. 'It was an ember tornado, like driving into hell,' Donna said.

The couple sought refuge in the nearby Moss Vale evacuation centre. They lost everything that night. 'There were just two chimneys left of our house,' she said. 'All we could really see in the mess was a couple of old kitchen bowls.' Three other houses on their street were also gutted.

Back in Wingello, the Stimson family successfully saved their home against ember attack. It was a terrifying ordeal for David. For more than 20 years, he had been a source of information and calm for the Southern Highlands community. As public information officer with the RFS, that summer his voice regularly sounded across ABC Radio, providing the latest emergency information to listeners.

But the speed and ferocity of the Currowan fire caught him, and everyone else, by surprise. 'To see a fire of such magnitude under southerly conditions was just unheard of,' he said. 'Fires that are driven by southerly winds are usually much cooler, and have a lot more humidity, but the fire behaviour we saw that night has rewritten the textbook.'

Jessie Davies is the features reporter for ABC Western Plains

Dark Days

Philip Williams and Greg Nelson

Wednesday, 1 January – Cobargo

It looks like 20 bulldozers have lined up and gouged a chaotic path through the centre of the historic town of Cobargo on the New South Wales south coast. There is a clear beginning and end to the destruction. And in between nothing but twisted roofing iron and the burnt fragments of people's businesses. The heart of the town is gone.

Cobargo residents Marylin Mills and Mick Thompson had moved into their Cobargo haven just before Christmas. It was a new start for both of them. A beautiful house on normally lush acreage, it was going to be a place for Marylin's five horses and three dogs to thrive, and had enough garage space to park Mick's collection of vintage cars. But just a few days later, their piece of heaven became a fiery hell. What looked like an easily controllable grass fire turned into a monster that overwhelmed the couple as they ran towards the shelter of the house. Blinded by the ash, Marylin couldn't find the front door and stumbled and fell.

'When I was lying there, I just had my hand out and I was trying to crawl over a bush and I just was screaming, "Mick! Mick! Mick!",' Marylin says. 'And I just thought, I am going to die.'

Mick heard her screams and ran back to help her. 'I had to run through the house to get to Marylin and I honestly thought that she would be on fire when I got back to her,' Mick recalls.

He managed to grab Marylin and drag her into the house, but it was already on fire. Marylin made a desperate call to triple zero and spoke to an operator, but was quickly interrupted. 'While he was still on the phone,' Marylin says, 'all the windows exploded in and so I started screaming and he said, "I will let the RFS know you are there."' She says the operator spoke in a calm, clear voice. 'He was so nice, but he just said, "Try and get a wet towel," and I said, "Well, we are dying." And he just said, "Well, you're on your own."'

They were about to become a statistic. Another two humans burnt to death in a horror season. But Mick had other ideas. He dragged Marylin and the three dogs into the adjacent garage hoping it might withstand the searing heat.

'I was lying in front of the cars, with my nose on the concrete just sucking in air,' says Marylin. 'The dogs panicked and got away from me. They went under the cars.'

Mick Thompson and Marylin Mills at their home in Cobargo, NSW.
(Greg Nelson/ABC)

Liz Lacey, centre, waiting at the Cobargo evacuation centre.
(Greg Nelson/ABC)

As she lay there expecting to die, Marylin made another two calls. The first to a friend to say goodbye. The second to triple zero. 'And I just said, "We're dying,"' Marylin recalls. 'And then all of a sudden it went completely quiet. There was no roar of the fire. The window went completely black. I was hysterical and then, right across both sides, the whole ceiling just became a fireball. And I remember Mick saying, "Bugger this, I'm not dying here." And next thing I know, he was dragging me over the top of the cars and dragging me out.'

Once in the open, they escaped in a four-wheeled buggy. The dogs didn't make it out. The horses, they found out later, were burnt but alive. So too were Mick and Marylin.

'It is the scariest thing and I would say to anyone out there – do not fight it,' says Marylin. 'Just get the hell out.'

—

At the makeshift evacuation centre on the Cobargo showground, shell-shocked evacuees have gathered together for sanctuary and support. Cooking food donated from local businesses that can no longer store it because the power is out, they keep a barbecue going and share with each other what little information they have on their situations.

Among them is Cobargo resident Scott Herring. Like Mick and Marylin, he and his family are fairly new to the area. He's working the barbecue, turning meat over on the hot plate, and the smoke is helping to hide the tears in his red eyes. 'It's shattering to see the main street,' he says. 'This is such a great little town and we've loved living here. Yeah, it's pretty crap. I feel for everyone.'

A firefighter for National Parks and Wildlife, Scott had been prepared to defend his new home in the bush. After earlier getting his family to safety he stood ready with a hose and pump but he was alone and, even with all his experience, he was no match for what came. 'As firefighters you work smart, you don't work stupid like trying to save a house. You put yourself out of harm's way … because it's not somewhere you should be.'

Scott had water – 2000 litres of it. 'It was enough to do the job,' he says, 'but it would have been real nice to have someone to help me with the hose. I couldn't move fast enough. These conditions were just unbelievable … The heat and the dryness and the winds, you know, no one could do anything about this. I made triple-zero calls but I didn't expect any help 'cause … you just … everyone's flat out everywhere, from here to Coffs Harbour or further.'

The fire consumed his sheds, his home and the kids' beloved chickens, and it sent the goats scattering in fear. All Scott managed to save was a single box from their recent move, labelled with his daughter's name, which he hastily filled with whatever he could throw from the house as it burnt. 'This place was [our kids'] new home, and they had all their stuff – Christmas presents and all that … just all their things, their little things that they loved. So I guess for them it's going to be real hard to come back.'

After the fire had passed through, he returned to the house to survey the devastation and gather up the frightened goats that had returned. There's feed for them at the showground, donated for the animals that could be saved.

'From what I've seen in this town,' Scott says, 'this is a town with one of the strongest communities I've ever come across. I'm really proud to live here. There's a lot of really good people in this town. It's gonna be a difficult time but I think if anywhere can do it and anywhere can pull through, then from what I've seen, Cobargo can do it.'

Despite the devastation, Scott is certain he and his family will stay in the area and rebuild. Besides, he says, where else are they going to go? This is their home. Choking back tears, he says, 'This is where we wanna be … We'll stay.'

—

Also at the showground, Liz Lacey sits on a bench with her friend Imi surrounded by fellow evacuees and various pet dogs, all waiting for news. Liz is desperately worried for the horses she had to leave behind. She hopes her home of 30 years has been spared but she fears the worst.

When she feels she's ready, she drives as close as she can to her property – until a fallen power pole blocks her path. From there, it's a walk along a burnt-out road. With every step comes a new glimpse of the devastation on her neighbours' properties. Hope is fast receding. 'Well, my shed's gone,' she says. 'I can see that.'

At her closed front gate, Liz spots a horse – it's alive but stranded in another paddock by fallen wires. It is blackened and hard to distinguish but she thinks it could be one of hers. She points towards the open fence next to her front gate. 'That's where the horses got out. Thank God for that.'

Turning back to her own property, the view is less promising. 'Can't see my roof but I can see my chimney,' she says. Pushing through the front gate and down the drive she is hoping for another miracle but it's not to be.

Her house is gone. Sheds and stables too. The awful shock sets in and the tears begin to flow. 'I can't believe it. I just can't believe it. I don't know what we're supposed to do next, I just don't know. I think we've just gotta get on with it, hey? It's gonna be hard but we have to do it. I'm not going anywhere. I'll rebuild again.'

It's a scene being repeated in towns up and down the New South Wales south coast. In nearby Quaama or further north at Mogo and Batemans Bay, residents are returning from evacuation centres and temporary shelters to confront their own devastation. In Cobargo they are grappling with the terrible loss of two of their neighbours, Robert and Patrick Salway. The grief is raw for everyone here.

'My heart's totally broken,' Liz says, 'but you've just gotta go on. Simple as that, hey? I suppose it's not that simple. It won't be that simple. But we'll do it and everybody else will and we've got a great community so we'll all help each other.'

Saturday, 4 January – Bega

Everyone is on high alert. The weather forecast and fire predictions are the worst they can be. Exhausted residents and firefighters are on edge. It's a terrible waiting game. In Bermagui, an hour up the coast, almost the entire town has retreated to the harbour, ready to evacuate by sea if the worst happens.

Evacuees at the Bega showground watch the sky, waiting for the forecast change in the wind to carry smoke and embers towards them. The tension is palpable. The fear raw.

By mid-afternoon, there's a sudden flurry of activity from emergency services on the edge of town. The fire front to the west of Bega along the Brown Mountain road is making a run. We head out with the fire trucks and the smoke begins rising higher and getting darker. As we reach the Numbugga fire shed, 15 kilometres from Bega, we encounter several firefighting vehicles retreating. A man on the back of one truck waves desperately for us to turn around. There's terror on his face.

Residents in the district are fleeing their farms. Others are staying put, waiting to fight the front as it races up the hill towards open ground.

Two fire trucks take up positions near the fire shed and run lines out to meet it head on. As they begin to douse spot fires that are flaring up, one firefighter stumbles from exhaustion, slamming his head against a tree. He gets up, adjusts his helmet and goes straight back to dousing the flames. There's no time to rest or recover.

More trucks arrive and then a howling southerly wind blows through, whipping the trees wildly from side to side. The air is now thick with smoke and embers. Darkness falls at three in the afternoon. It will be days before we see the sun again. The front roars to life in the trees around us. The firies go to work, holding the line as the southerly wind change steers the fire back.

Saturday, 4 January – Eden

The air is not really air. It is a congested soup so thick with heavy ash particles that every breath feels like a slow drowning. The fires from Victoria have swept into southern New South Wales with a speed that has left the residents of the port town of Eden scrambling for safety. Many have chosen the main wharf, because, as a last resort, you can always dive into the bay to escape the flames. There are fishing boats crammed full of children and parents, ready to head into the bay if the flames come too close. And along the length of the wharf, huddled groups wearing makeshift protective clothing – ski goggles, builders' face masks, heads wrapped in scarves– anything to

Liz Lacey, above, seeing the remains of her house, below. (Greg Nelson/ABC)

protect them from a world that has turned very nasty very quickly. Everyone is wondering if their homes will survive, fretting about relatives and friends, pets and property.

These are fire refugees, frightened and disoriented, with no idea how this terror will end. For many it is the first time they have experienced such an existential threat to their world. This is a dystopian horror movie, set in a town named after paradise.

On a nearby sports oval, hundreds more residents are preparing their survival plan. There are no spare fire units, so they're on their own. They are all on the southern flank trying to stop the firestorm pushing into the town. Spontaneously, a dads' army fire protection unit is formed and a former soldier is elected mayor. They draw a black line on the oval, making the decision to defend everything behind it. A couple of 1000-litre plastic cubes on trailers are set up. If the red beast comes, the people on the oval will be sheltered by a protective shower from the hoses. And if that fails, the beach is just a short sprint away.

For hours they wait in eerie darkness, spirits kept buoyant with that old combination of jokes and beer. It could have been every man, woman and child for themselves. Instead, this is community in action looking after each other.

We drive out of Eden at 1 am and discover the fire front is just a short distance away at Boydtown. For the next twelve hours, we are the only media reporting from here. Everything we do is being broadcast across the ABC, on TV, radio and the web. We feel a responsibility to be here, to tell the evacuees' stories and to help keep them informed.

Back in Eden, as thick ash falls from the sky and smoke hangs heavy in the glare of floodlights by the wharf, everyone looks for somewhere to wait out the night in safety. With power out and generators humming, many have gathered inside the Wharfside Café. No one expected the situation here in Eden to be this threatening so soon. They're huddled inside, silent and tired, listening intently to ABC Radio's emergency broadcast for any information on the homes and towns they've hurriedly left behind. The news is not good.

After having covered the situation in Bermagui, Bega, Tathra, Cobargo and Numbugga all Saturday, we are exhausted. There's no respite from the choking smoke-filled air. Greta Asojanovic from the Wharfside Café offers us a spot on her kitchen floor to rest our heads. We file our last report at 3 am and we're both so very grateful for a few hours' sleep before we have to roll out again at 5 am and head south to the devastated bush village of Kiah, five kilometres south.

In the café, the sound of ABC Radio continues to offer information and comfort for those too anxious to sleep.

Sunday, 5 January – Eden

It's difficult to convey just how disorienting the never-ending night is. Morning comes, but not the light. The smoke and ash are so thick that the certainty of day following night is simply not there. The total dark, smudged with a menacing red glow, hangs over Eden and far beyond for more than a day.

The fire front has swept through Kiah and the village is still smouldering. On our return to Eden, we go again to the wharf where we find Adam Fleeton and his partner, who are seeking refuge there, having fled from their home in Kiah yesterday. We tell them the bush is burning in all directions. The very reason people like Adam chose to live there – the beautiful trees – is now the reason their homes, the local church and the hall have not survived. The Kiah general store has survived, we tell them, but it is little comfort.

Adam is almost certain his beloved bush home is going to be just another pile of twisted metal roofing. 'The way the fire went through there,' he says, 'there's no chance our house would have survived. We're just expecting to go back to nothing, but we've got all our personal photos and stuff like that.' He is grateful that he and his partner have each other. 'That's the main thing. As long as lives are spared, that's all we're worried about. We'll get through.'

It is rare to end an interview with a hug, but that's what happens after we finish speaking to Adam – strangers uniting in a long deep expression of raw grief. These fires have burnt away social niceties and barriers. We all share the same fears. In this moment, we are not teachers, mayors, fishermen, mothers or fathers, but all frightened humans stripped bare of position,

Scott Herring. (Greg Nelson/ABC)

The remains of Scott Herring's house and shed. (Greg Nelson/ABC)

authority and pretension. There is one shared goal. To survive. And all in the endless darkness.

As journalists covering this disaster we sometimes feel like interlopers, members of an out-of-town crew rushing in to report on other people's tragedies. We don't belong here, but our colleagues at ABC Local live here. This is their community. They know these people. One journalist is in tears in the newsroom after a night spent protecting their home and offering sanctuary to others who have fled theirs. They live with the impact and its effects every day, and will continue to do so long after the spotlight has moved on.

Philip Williams is the ABC's chief foreign correspondent

Greg Nelson ACS is a NSW-based cinematographer working for ABC News and 7.30

Battling On

Casey Briggs

'Everything's gone about as badly as possible and about as well as can be expected.'

The third and final round of severe bushfires on Kangaroo Island had finally been tamed, and Kangaroo Island's mayor Michael Pengilly was addressing reporters at Kingscote Town Hall. He was concise but brutal.

'We've done our best and the best hasn't been good enough, but we battle on.'

—

When I first met Peter Davis on 6 January, he was a man on the brink of exhaustion. He'd just been to the post office, the bank and the police station, where he'd filed a report on some suspected looters at his family's property.

Kynan Lang mourning his uncle Dick and cousin Clayton, who died in early January 2020 on the Playford Highway in Kangaroo Island, SA. (Brittany Evins/ABC)

The beekeeper was running on fumes and mourning his devastated business, choking back tears as we talked. He had been managing around 1200 beehives and after the first wave of fires in late December, he'd moved a third of them to the relative safety of Kingscote, the island's largest town.

On 3 January, the fires flared again. Around 500 of Peter's remaining 800 hives in the field were destroyed, and many of those that survived were structurally weakened. Most were full of honey yet to be harvested.

Peter led me and camera operator Carl Saville on a drive deep into the western end of Kangaroo Island to show us the damage. He showed us where firefighters were continuing their hard work, backburning in a paddock to protect the small pockets of vegetation and national park that hadn't already been burnt. In a plantation only a few hundred metres to the west, Peter had 150 beehives among the trees. If the plantation went up, Peter expected to lose those hives too.

As it turned out, he was right. Despite the firefighters' best efforts, only around three of those survived.

We drove further inland, passing once-vibrant forests that were now monochromatic, and then turned onto his son's property. Peter and his family had sheltered in the house while the blaze roared around them. The structure kept them safe for long enough for the fire to pass, but it suffered too much damage and later collapsed.

'My two sons and I, we survived in a house that no longer exists,' Peter said.

Most of his son's sheep didn't survive either, and the few dozen that did had to be sent to market. What was left was a shadow of the house that once stood there. Spilling across the charred ground were signs of a lost livelihood.

The ashy soil among the rubble was sticky. We were looking at what was left of a stockpile of honey, ready for sale.

'That would have been, like, 600 to 900 kilograms,' Peter explained. 'It is just literally a pool down the road.'

As we pulled up to what was left of one set of beehives, a huge flock of birds lifted off in formation from the ground, darting into the surrounding black trunks.

I couldn't recall seeing any living wildlife in hours, but we found ourselves dodging birds swooping from branches and hopping around our feet. With the forests completely burnt, the birds were congregating around the only source of food they could find: dribbles of honey spilling out from the damaged hives. They were desperately pecking at any sustenance they could spot.

The lack of plant life would make Peter's efforts at rebuilding difficult as well. No foliage meant no flowers, no nectar, and no pollen for the bees.

'We've lost probably 90 per cent of the available resources for our bees in this one day,' Peter told me. 'A lot of these trees won't flower for up to seven years.'

Burnt beehives on Kangaroo Island. (Casey Briggs/ABC)

Peter Davis checking on his beehives. (Carl Saville/ABC)

The surviving bees would be fed with sugar syrup and a protein supplement, dispensed from bee-feeder troughs.

'It's going to be very difficult for a very long time,' he said. Yet, despite how hard he'd been hit, Peter's resolve was strong. 'We have a community spirit here on Kangaroo Island that is not burnable.'

Peter paused as the emotion of the past few days caught up with him.

'It hurts. It hurts to see this, and I don't want anyone to go through this again. We will work together, we will survive, we will get stronger. Don't give up on Kangaroo Island because we're not gonna give up.'

Of course, Peter wasn't to know at the time just how hard 2020 would get. Four months later, I spoke to him again on the phone.

Just as Kangaroo Islanders had cleared enough wreckage and were ready to welcome visitors again, bringing much-needed cash to the local economy, they found themselves shooing people away as a pandemic swept across the globe.

The cruel irony was that a major advertising campaign to bring tourists back was just starting to have an impact. Peter had just stocked up on Easter products to sell through his gift shop when he was forced to shut.

But as we talked, I sensed that there was more Peter wanted to tell me. He's a stoic man, but it was clear that the scars of

January 2020 had cut deep. He struggled to find the words and – like the first day we'd met – choked up.

After a long pause he confided in me that he'd made an appointment to see a counsellor. 'It's very hard to admit that you're not coping,' he said. 'But I'm not ashamed of it. I just find it very hard to talk about. I think we're just lucky that we haven't had anyone that's suicided so far.'

While he'd kept busy rebuilding the parts of the business he could control, Peter had not been back out to the western end of the island, the site of all the damage, in the four months since we first met.

'I've never felt like this before,' he said.

He's not alone.

—

The fires that took over Australia's third-largest island were dramatic and devastating, and – because of the catastrophic effect on national parks and wildlife – drew international attention. It was the worst way to end an already bad summer in South Australia.

By the time the fires were extinguished, 89 homes had been destroyed, another 11 had suffered major damage, and 268 other buildings – like farming sheds and warehouses – were also gone. And two people had died: Dick and Clayton Lang perished on the highway as they returned from battling fire on the island.

The fire burnt through 210,000 hectares and had a perimeter of at least 595 kilometres.

As firefighters frantically made plans, wildlife park operators were moving their animals to safety, and farmers were preparing to defend their properties.

Daniel Haby was among them, busily moving cattle to bare paddocks, setting up a sprinkler pointed directly at his shearing shed, and cleaning up his yard. Plumes of black smoke in the distance rolled towards him. He was worried about a fierce, wide fire front.

'There's the big Parndana Conservation Park just on our boundary,' he told me. 'It hasn't been burnt for 30 years so, yeah, we're expecting it to be quite extreme.'

Firefighters knew the weather conditions would make the afternoon tricky, but when a wind change blew in earlier than expected, fears grew for homes and towns far further to the east than had been initially thought at risk.

By six o'clock, conditions were so unpredictable that firefighters were considering placing the entirety of Kangaroo Island under an emergency warning. That would've been a major declaration, one that likely would have sparked a stampede of locals and visitors to evacuate the island.

There was a sense of chaos at the firefighters' base camp, as plans were rapidly made. The defence force constructed firebreaks around the campsite, and equipment and personnel were pulled back from the fire front.

The situation continued to escalate through the night.

A large emergency alert was issued around half past midnight, catching residents to the west of Kingscote by surprise. Some quickly loaded up their cars or caravans and drove into town – where at least they could be sure of their safety – and settled in for a long night on the oval, or down by the jetty. Some were trying to get a little bit of rest in their cars and caravans. Others didn't sleep a wink.

Nineteen-year-old Kate Heinrich took shelter at the shore. She had been sent to Kingscote from her family's sheep farm near Stokes Bay by relatives who had stayed to defend the property.

'I spent my birthday yesterday in Kingscote, thinking this was the safest place on the island,' Kate said. 'We were just freaking out, so late last night we just packed up the house that I was staying in … I haven't slept at all.'

It was a long night. Around two in the morning, she heard that the winds were pushing flames back towards her family's property.

'We've just been hanging in the car waiting and waiting for news,' she said.

That news eventually did come, as the sun started to rise. The flames came right to the edge of the farm, but it had been saved.

Later in the day, after roads had reopened, we drove back to Daniel Haby's farm to see how he'd fared. While residents had evacuated further east, Daniel had managed to keep the flames at bay. Remarkably his sheds had barely been scarred.

'It was quite ferocious, the fire front coming through,' he said. 'The flames would have been 50 or 60 metres high and making a lot of noise. It was like being down the ocean when there's a storm coming in. Lots of cracking and crashing and banging. It just jumped all fire breaks and there was nothing that could be done to stop it.'

He did what he could to extinguish spot fires on his land, but eventually the heat was so intense he retreated to safety. 'I've got quite a leafy mulberry tree beside my shed and I'd sprayed that all down with water,' he said. 'There was about a ten-minute period where I hid underneath the mulberry tree.'

I looked up at the towering tree in disbelief that it would offer much protection from a fast-moving bushfire. But its many layers of leaves, low to the ground, offered just the refuge he needed.

'I knew that if there were ember fires coming through – showers of ember sparks – that would be a very safe place to be, underneath the wet leaves of the mulberry tree.'

Remarkably, all he ended up losing were around 200 hay bales and most of his fencing: by no means trivial to replace, but far from the worst-case scenario.

Many stockowners were not as lucky. Across the island 32,000 head of stock were lost in the fires, causing some of the grimmest scenes of destruction. Farmers grieving the loss of their properties and their livelihoods were forced back out onto the land to dispose of the animals. The job took priority even over sifting through the remains of flattened properties. Everyone pitched in to get the job done quickly before it became a major biosecurity issue.

But it still took a very long time. Four days after the destruction, we were still driving past trucks and tractors loaded with carcasses on their way to be buried in freshly dug graves.

—

While Kangaroo Island captured the most international attention in the summer of 2019–20, other parts of South Australia also suffered greatly. Serious fires affected Yorke Peninsula, the southeast, and mid-north of the state. But the state's second scene of major devastation was the Adelaide Hills.

A fire that started on a chaotic day at Cudlee Creek on 20 December quickly spread, destroying 86 homes and claiming one life. It burnt through around a third of the Adelaide Hills' vineyards at a remarkable pace. The damage forced one dairy to throw out tens of thousands of kilograms of now-inedible cheese. It directly impacted towns in the Adelaide Hills including Gumeracha and Woodside. At one point residents in Lobethal could see nothing in the sky but smoke as their township was attacked on all sides. By the time the fires were out, the town was nearly encircled by burnt land.

The Cudlee Creek fire was declared contained on New Year's Eve, after burning through just under 24,000 hectares within a 185-kilometre perimeter.

The summer of 2019–20 was the busiest summer of my journalistic career to date. I'd covered many disasters, cyclones and tragedies, but no natural disaster that was as relentless, surprising or long-lasting as this bushfire crisis.

The resilience and positive attitude people had, even while staring at a wreck of burnt materials where their house had once stood, were remarkable. And I was in awe of firefighters across the country who dropped everything to help, camping out on long rotations to keep people safe.

For people like Peter, Daniel and Kate, the wounds from the bushfires still cut deep. It will take a long time for everyone touched by the fires to recover. But just like in nature, as green shoots sprout across the landscape, the wounds will eventually heal.

Even when things go about as badly as possible, Australians dust themselves off and battle on.

Casey Briggs is a journalist for ABC News in Sydney

A summer like no other. All along the southeast coast of Australia, people nervously holidayed while fires raged around them – here looking out from Moruya Heads, NSW, on New Year's Eve. (Mary Rennie)

Catastrophic conditions. By 21 January 2020, more than half of Kangaroo Island, SA, was burnt. (Brittany Evins/ABC)

As fires raged in every state and territory, Australian firefighters were helped by teams flown in from New Zealand, Canada, Singapore and the United States. (Brendan Esposito/ABC)

Large plumes of smoke from bushfires can become pyrocumulus clouds, creating their own weather patterns and making hazardous conditions even more unpredictable. (Brendan Esposito/ABC)

Gabo Island, against a backdrop of smoke from Mallacoota, Victoria. By early January, smoke from the Australian bushfires had drifted to South America. (Jonathon Kendall)

On New Year's Eve, the main street of Cobargo, NSW, was engulfed by an emergency-level fire.
(Above: Brendan Esposito/ABC; below: Matt Roberts/ABC; right: Greg Nelson/ABC)

COBARGO

Dark days. Thousands sought shelter at Eden wharf on 4 January, prepared to dive into the sea if necessary. (Greg Nelson/ABC)

Firefighting helicopters grounded by thick smoke at Merimbula airport. (Greg Nelson/ABC)

ABC journalists reporting from the front line. Left to right: Jeremy Fernandez at Rosedale, NSW (David Sciasci/ABC); Greg Nelson filming at Numbugga, NSW (Philip Williams/ABC); Lily Mayers at Gospers Mountain, NSW (Peter Drought/ABC).

The fickle nature of fires means that a house can be razed while two plastic wheelie bins survive. Aerial view of a destroyed home and surrounding burnt forest in the Southern Highlands, NSW. (Brendan Esposito/ABC)

A heavy toll. Volunteer firefighters worked tirelessly in life-threatening conditions. (Brendan Esposito/ABC)

ABC journalist Matthew Doran reporting from Dartmouth Dam, near Corryong, Victoria. (Steve Opie/ABC)

Wytaliba Public School in northern NSW, one of the thousands of buildings gutted by the fires. (Josh Bavas/ABC)

The burnt forest surrounding Bundanon Homestead in Illaroo, NSW. (Brendan Esposito/ABC)
Opposite page: an injured koala in the Adelaide Hills, SA (Brittany Evins/ABC); scorched sheep in Batlow, NSW (Matt Roberts/ABC); a burnt horse in Cobargo, NSW (Greg Nelson/ABC).
The fires tore through an estimated 18.6 million hectares across Australia, killing or displacing up to three billion animals. Some endangered native species might never recover.

Adriane Reardon reporting from Eden wharf at 10 am, 5 January 2020. (Adriane Reardon)

Is this the new normal? (Greg Nelson/ABC)

EVACUATION

Like in many coastal towns, the surf club in Bermagui is the hub and heart of the community. On sunny summer days, families and friends pop in and out of the clubhouse – spending their days swimming, playing, chatting.

But on the morning of New Year's Eve, 2019, it was a refuge for more than 5000 people, many of whom had just fled their homes as the fire bore down on their communities inland. Three surf club volunteers were already setting up by the time I arrived. We hugged each other – all dry in the throat and wide-eyed.

People started piling in soon after. A woman from Yowrie walked in with three small children, all in their pyjamas, and asked me if she could bring her cat inside from her car. Before I could respond, words and tears started spilling out of her. 'I just watched my house burn down,' she said. 'Everything is gone.'

I looked her in the eyes and then down at her children. I felt like there was nothing I could say or do in that moment that would ease her pain.

She spoke again, louder this time. 'It's gone. We saw it burn down,' she said. She was angry now. 'Where can I take my cat?' She started yelling. 'We don't have insurance! Where are we going to live?' She was screaming.

I blurted out an apology and pathetically offered her water and a cup of tea. I'll never forget the pain in that woman's eyes for as long as I live.

Hours passed as I ushered people into the club and asked them to sign in. It was a surreal blur of faces – both familiar and strange – all united by intense fear. Cheryl, the club secretary, sensed my increasing distress and tasked me to a solitary job away from the stream of evacuees pouring in. As I sat upstairs in the clubhouse, entering people's details into a database, I turned the scanner back on. It was then that I heard it: a firefighter seeking instruction from Firecom about a family with several children, huddled together in one house. Flames had already started licking the veranda.

'Just save life only,' was the RFS radio reply.

'Grab the children, just grab all the children,' the firefighter yelled to his crew.

I stood up, feeling dizzy and nauseous, and ran out of the clubhouse with an overwhelming and desperate need to find Yannis.

Claire Wheaton

Smoke from the Mogo fire as it swept towards Broulee, NSW. (Mary Rennie)

Disaster Unfolds Live On Air

Melinda James

It was just before 7 am on New Year's Day. Lyn was on the line from Milton, live to air on ABC Illawarra. 'Hi Mel, I'm calling from the old phone box on the Princes Highway in Milton. The phone won't accept coins but I could call your ABC 1300 number for free. It's the only way to get through.'

Car horns were beeping in the background. Lyn said there was a bank-up of cars trying to head north but they weren't going anywhere – the road was closed. There was no power, no fuel, no ice. Mobile reception was virtually non-existent. The previous day the fire had reached the Catholic school on the northern outskirts of town before a southerly change had sent the flames north. The change was fantastic for Milton but would have been devastating for Lake Conjola and Yatte Yattah, just ten kilometres away.

In the studio, we were stunned. Milton is surrounded by pasture and cleared land. It's prime dairy country. How did the fire get so close?

It's smoky and eerie, Lyn said. People are desperate; there's no way out.

That morning, everyone was hungry for information. I was back on air after nine hours broadcasting from ABC Illawarra the day before, on a chaotic New Year's Eve, when soaring temperatures and a powerful early southerly had sent the Currowan fire raging up the New South Wales coast. Shocking images flowed in from further south – Malua Bay, Mogo, Cobargo and Batemans Bay were either ablaze or already destroyed. Lives had been lost, we knew that for sure. But we weren't sure how many homes had been destroyed and feared it would certainly be in the hundreds.

Our last on-air moments of 2019 had been spent talking to people from the small villages and suburbs further north in the Shoalhaven – Yatte Yattah, Little Forest, Conjola Park. With power and phone lines down, details were scant. Come the morning, calls flooded in from around the country.

Fran in Tasmania grew up in Yatte Yattah. 'Is there any news?' she pleaded. 'My heart is breaking.'

Yvonne was in tears. Her daughter was in Conjola.

Jenny's grandson was there too. She was frantic.

Another Jenny in Adelaide: her family was also at Lake Conjola. 'This is a bloody disaster,' she yelled down the phone. 'Why aren't they sending in cruise ships to pick people up? They're running out of food.'

—

A radio studio can be a lonely place. Sometimes you wonder if anyone's even listening. But never had I felt the presence of listeners like I did through the peak of this fire. Trust had been built over an already terrible summer and people now felt ownership of the radio. They didn't just passively listen – they used us. ABC Radio stopped being 'the media' and became the community square. A place to talk to each other, share vital information, ask for help, vent, rage. We were a megaphone to warn neighbours the fire was approaching and, when the immediate danger had passed, we were a shoulder to cry on – or cry with. Some callers were lost for words, couldn't speak. Their voices might have been cracking but they didn't get off the phone. They needed to talk, feel connected. And there was a palpable sense that thousands of people were leaning in, listening intently, gripped by harrowing accounts of fire bearing down … or, later, sharing the grief of someone who had just lost everything.

It's also rare as a broadcaster to be hearing information for the first time as it goes to air. But this emergency was playing out in real time, live on the radio. There was no crafting and repackaging of information, no censoring or editing of people's emotions. And there was no time to temper my own. It was raw and real and moving fast. In those dark days between New Year's Eve and 5 January, with information hard to come by, the intimacy and immediacy of radio came into its own. Which was lucky, because with no power, no internet and unreliable phone reception, a battery-powered radio or the car stereo was all some people had.

—

Information started to flow on New Year's Day, largely thanks to listeners. Tens of thousands of holidaymakers were stranded. Fire was everywhere in the landscape. The Roads and Traffic Authority's live traffic website showed thick red lines on all major roads: the Kings Highway linking Canberra to the coast was closed, the Princes Highway to the north was blocked between Milton and Nowra, and there was no going south from Batemans Bay. Smaller local roads, the only way out of the tiny villages just off the highway were also shut. There was no way out for the foreseeable future. But these people needed to get home – they were being told to get out. An even worse forecast was looming: in three days we were expecting temperatures in the mid-40s and, if that wasn't enough, a violent southerly buster, a set of bellows to push the fire north towards more townships.

Callers told us that staff at the Milton IGA were wearing head torches and leading customers around one at a time to get basic supplies. At Ulladulla, larger than Milton and a few kilometres south, Woolworths was the only place in the area with generator power – and listeners described a mob gathering outside. As word got out, the queue to get in stretched for blocks. Woollies was out of candles. Batteries, long-life milk and bread were running low and locals called in angry that people were walking out with full trolleys. 'We're gonna *need* that stuff,' they told us.

Still, a vital question hung in the air unanswered – what had happened at Conjola?

The ABC's Selby Stewart was the first reporter into Conjola Park, a small suburb just off the highway, overlooking Lake Conjola. He arrived at 5 am as the sun was coming up over the smouldering ruins of the town. When we finally got him on air via a satellite phone, he described an apocalypse.

'The street signs have all melted,' Selby said. 'There are cars on the street that have melted. The paint's dripped and solidified on the road.' He counted at least 40 houses completely destroyed. There were certainly many more in areas he couldn't reach. He found people at first light, dazed and calling out for lost pets, searching though rubble to make sure everyone was accounted for. 'It's really …' For a moment, words escaped him. 'The community's really hurting down here.'

Selby recounted what he'd heard from those who had stayed to defend their homes. 'The fire was so intense, it became a firestorm. It was pitch-black. The winds were so strong and there were embers flying everywhere.'

People had described to him the sickening sound of animals howling in distress. The horror was so immense, they told him, that if they had their time over, they would not have stayed. Bugger the house, never again.

Selby later told me he had been stopped on arrival by a deeply traumatised and desperate man. 'I can't find my elderly neighbour,' the man had said. 'She was here. We don't know where she is.' Selby helped the man trawl through the ruins and ashes of his neighbour's home. It wasn't until that night he heard her family had come and got her out with 20 minutes to spare.

Straight after Selby's report, a listener named Hayley called in from Ulladulla with an update on what was happening at Woollies. She wouldn't recommend trying to get in, she said, the queues were enormous.

I asked if she was local. She said, 'Yep, I'm from Conjola Park.' It was a jolt that caught me in the guts. We fell into silence. Chances were high she had been listening to Selby's report while she was on hold. She told me the last she'd heard before she got out was that her front and back yards were on fire. 'It happened within an hour.' More silence. All I could say was, 'I'm so sorry, Hayley. So sorry.'

—

Slowly, more stories emerged of what had happened at Conjola.

Just before 11 am on New Year's Eve, Brett Cripps had been on the roof of the holiday house he'd been coming to for 50 years, filling the gutters with water. He saw a plume of smoke not far off. At 11.04 am he put a message on Facebook to warn neighbours the fire was coming. A little over half an hour later embers were flying, causing spot fires all around.

'It just went up within minutes,' Brett told us. 'Hit the first house. The second house. Hit our house. A fourth house.' He ran down to his jetty and took his boat to the middle of the lake. He saw spot fires 'going berserk' on the opposite shore near two young families and their caravans. They were about to get in their cars to try to escape. He screamed at them, 'Get in the boat, get in the boat! I don't care how you get in, just get in.'

His five-metre boat, built to hold six people, soon had 15 on board, including seven children under ten. Within minutes their nearby cars and caravans were incinerated. For nearly three hours, along with dozens of other overloaded boats and jet skis bobbing on Lake Conjola, they watched as houses burnt. Mini tornados whipped burning leaves and embers into the air. Trees cracked and gas bottles popped. Brett was proud of the kids. 'They were crying at first,' he said. 'But then they were quiet. Really just … quiet.'

Shoalhaven mayor Amanda Findley was at the Ulladulla Civic Centre, an evacuation centre powered by generators borrowed from, of all places, a visiting circus. 'When the news came in from Conjola, it just felt like the blood was draining from your body,' she said later. 'It was like a slow burn.' One family after another, after another. 'And they're all people you know.'

Two staff members from the Milton IGA had lost their homes at Conjola Park. Their boss, Shane Wilson, said they turned up to work the next day, one of them in the only clothes she had left. 'She had a small pair of gumboots on because she had no shoes,' Shane said. 'A customer come to me and gives me $50 and says, "Can you make sure that young girl gets that money for a pair of shoes?"'

The final count was 89 homes destroyed at Conjola Park.

'This has been life shattering,' Shane told us. 'And unfortunately we've lost a few valuable people.' He broke down and couldn't continue on air.

Three local men had died. But there was no time to grieve, not yet.

Mark Williams, incident controller for the Currowan fire, had bad news. 'We are expecting a similar if not worse day [on 4 January] than we had on New Year's Eve,' he said. 'We are imploring people: if they don't need to be here, as soon as they can get out they should do so.'

Right: **Long queues of cars trying to leave Cobargo, NSW.** (Matt Roberts/ABC)

Below: **ABC journalist Selby Stewart interviewing Eurobodalla Shire Mayor Liz Innes, Batemans Bay.** (Timothy Swanston/ABC)

Over the coming days, evacuating tourists became the priority. But the ongoing threat of fire and falling trees meant fire-ravaged seaside villages were completely cut off. Local roads opened to the Princes Highway, then closed again. The highway itself opened, then closed again. It was difficult to keep up. Police escorted a few cars out at a time.

And the calls kept coming.

Neil phoned in and said people were panicking at Sussex Inlet. There was a three-kilometre queue to get into a service station where fuel had finally arrived. But, tank empty or full, no one could get out anyway.

Michael called. He reckoned 3000 people were trying to get out of Lake Conjola. People with young kids had been sitting in their cars for 24 hours and people were starting to ration food.

Bruce gave instructions to anyone listening on how to get into his caravan at Conjola, where there was a stack of food. He'd fled just before New Year's Eve because his place near Tallong in the Southern Highlands was under threat from the northern flank of this massive fire. 'Please, go inside and help yourself,' he said.

A logjam of cars and caravans stretched 20 kilometres south from Milton. People waiting for the highway north to open were refusing to budge for fear of losing their spot, preferring to sleep by the side of the side of the road. Caravans and cars occupied every inch of the town.

Layla called in and told us that locals had put signs in their gardens offering their bathrooms to travellers. Others were making people cups of tea. Kids were cycling up and down the highway, giving out bottles of water.

Mayor Findley said her daughter's boyfriend had ridden past a seemingly endless stretch of cars bumper to bumper – and he'd heard ABC Radio leaking out of every car stereo.

The Princes Highway to the north of Milton winds through thickly forested national parks, with the occasional turn-off to remote villages or bushy campgrounds. It's usually an idyllic and peaceful drive, but flames were still flickering and embers glowing by the side of the road, threatening to flare and again isolate communities. Crews worked all night to fell hundreds of smouldering trees, repair power lines and ensure the roads were safe. Eventually, good news started to trickle in. Roads were opening. People called with reassuring tales of progress. Be patient, they said, you'll get a clear run if you can make it to Nowra.

Polly called to say she'd made it home – 23 hours from Batemans Bay to Sydney listening to ABC Radio all the way. The same trip would usually take about four hours. For tens of thousands of holidaymakers, a terrifying ordeal was finally coming to an end. But for locals, the horror forecast of the next day loomed like a dark finale.

—

Early on 4 January, it was already stinking hot. I'd swapped the morning shift for the late afternoon to get some much-needed sleep ahead of my eighth day in a row of broadcasting. But today felt different. There were only locals left. We could feel people bracing. Evacuation centres were filling. Everybody just to the north of the Currowan fire's flank knew it would eventually jump the Shoalhaven River and head their way. One resident of Kangaroo Valley said it was like being sentenced to death but not being told the date of your execution. Finally, the time had come for the community to stare this fire down.

By now well-practised, listeners started calling in to share information. It was 47 degrees at Fisherman's Paradise; 51 at Kangaroo Valley. White ash was raining on Callala Bay. In Nowra, day became night within minutes. Winds from the east and west collided, creating a convection effect. An enormous pyrocumulus storm appeared on the Bureau of Meteorology radar as a red and black mass about 60 kilometres long. By this point in the summer, Australians were all too familiar with these fire-induced storms, or flammagenitus cloud. They dramatically increase the risk of fire spread, generating dry lightning strikes and wild, erratic winds that can fling embers for kilometres in all directions.

The alert went out at 4 pm. All residents on both sides of the Princes Highway from Nowra to Kioloa, 100 kilometres south, were told to 'shelter in place'. A similar warning was issued between Berry and Kangaroo Valley to its west. The entire

Shoalhaven region – 100,000 people – was told: wherever you are, it's too late to leave.

The calls flowed in. People were frustrated we couldn't tell them exactly where the fire was and where it was heading. There were fingers of fire front and new spot fires everywhere. The winds were so erratic, the air so hot and dry, that nowhere was safe.

Grant was well known to us, having called in several times back in early December with harrowing real-time reports of defending his property at Termeil, inland and a little south of Milton. From his vantage point up on the hill, he now described three massive columns of smoke edging their way towards coastal villages.

Chris in coastal Manyana could see flames 50 metres from his house. Water-bombing choppers were circling overheard. He was quite literally under fire, but Chris stayed cool, choosing to talk to ABC Radio. 'It's a bit of chaos here,' he said. 'As soon as the southerly hits we'll be right. Until then we're a bit stuffed.'

I told him he sounded pretty calm, as the wind whipped over the mouthpiece of his phone.

'Well, Mel,' he replied, 'you lose your head, you lose your life.' Finally, with the fire in his immediate vicinity, he just had to go.

We'd got word some fishermen from Ulladulla had spent the day delivering supplies by boat to communities cut off by fire and were now rescuing people from the beaches at

Manyana and Bendalong. Both communities were surrounded by fire. Producer Rory McDonald managed to get through to Ulladulla game fisher George Lirantzis who was on his boat, anchored just off the coast of Bendalong. George said he had room for some more people still stranded on the beach but the southerly had hit and it was too dangerous to head to shore again. 'These people have been to hell and back,' he said.

George handed his phone to a woman he'd just rescued. Gay had no idea she was now live on ABC Radio. I explained and apologised, but she said she didn't mind. 'I'm just over it,' she said of the fires, 'because it's been going for weeks and weeks and weeks. It's the southerly that got us this time.' She paused. 'Yeah, it's definitely going over my place at the moment.'

I imagined her craning her head and gazing in the direction of her house, watching the flames surround it. Then she laughed. 'I'm soaking wet with bare feet and I don't know where I'm going. But I'll be fine. I'll be fine.' To this day I'm astounded by how people like Gay let us into their most vulnerable moments live on air.

Back on land, the southerly seemed to be gathering pace as it hurtled north. For some it was a reprieve; for others almost certain devastation.

Gerard in Lake Tabourie rang in to say that the southerly had eased the threat at his place. I told him I'd lost count of the number of times the fire had menaced Lake Tabourie this summer. Gerard chuckled and told me he was going to sleep on the veranda with the hose in his hand.

It was approaching 8 pm and my shift was coming to end. I was on the line with Superintendent Mark Williams. After weeks of talking to this unflappable firefighter with 35 years' experience, a man who fights fires in the US and Canada in our off-season, this was the first time I'd heard his voice quicken. He told us the fire had crossed the Shoalhaven River to the north in several places. Fireballs were being flung north faster and further than anyone expected.

I told everyone listening to stay safe and look after one another, and then signed off. Colleagues told me to go home and rest. Don't listen to the radio, they said. Were they kidding? I tuned in to the radio in bed late into the night. Fitzroy Falls, a village inland not far from my mother-in-law's home, was ordered to shelter in place as the fire approached. Within a few hours, it was clear more homes had been lost in Kangaroo Valley and also in Wingello and Bundanoon, the latter not even mentioned in earlier warnings. We had thought it was too far from the fire front.

—

The relentlessness of this Currowan fire is still difficult to convey. Since it began one hot day in late November, sparked by a dry lightning strike in a remote state forest, it had terrorised the Shoalhaven again and again, circling around its hills and cleaves. Lives had been lost; hundreds of homes too. Some communities were evacuated two, three or four times. It was dubbed 'the never-ending fire'.

But it did end. We'd been told from the start that nothing could put this fire out but sustained and heavy rain. Finally, mercifully, rain came, rain like we hadn't seen for years. By 9 February the fire was out, 74 days after it started, having burnt through almost half-a-million hectares. In a cruel twist of fate, that same rain flooded Lake Conjola and damaged lakeside holiday homes where families who'd lost their properties to fire had been staying.

It was several weeks before I could see the damage for myself. By then the epicormic growth on the dominant eucalypt species had sprouted. Iridescent green shoots burst out along the lengths of limbs. They were a defiant, triumphant display of life in a blackened landscape that stretched as far as the eye could see. Some proud gums had shed their charred bark to reveal white trunks, almost glowing among the blackened stumps around them.

They reminded me of the people I'd met who had lost their homes. Many told me they'd been glued to the radio; despite never having met them before, these people felt like old friends. Stripped of everything, they stood tall, indefatigable.

Rod Hayes, who on 3 December became the first person to lose his home in the Currowan fire, also lost his extensive art collection and thousands of books. An architect in his 70s, he's now working on an underground fireproof design for a home carved into Boyne Mountain, dug into the same hill where his old place once stood.

At 84, Max Atkins, a former mayor of the Shoalhaven, narrowly escaped death when his Yatte Yattah home went up in flames. A couple of weeks after the fire, he returned to the ashes of his property to find tiny shoots sprouting from his lovingly tended but recently scorched rose garden. Painstakingly, he resurrected those roses and just two months later he took out a swag of blue and red ribbons for Best Rose at the Milton Show.

In Kangaroo Valley, long-time resident Chris Pryor showed me a lump of molten glass that used to be three Pyrex cooking bowls. It's all that remained of her home. She begged people to consider whether they could withstand the horror of living through a fire that liquifies material designed to melt at 1500 degrees. Are you really ready to defend your property?

Greg Webb had tried to save his family's place overlooking Lake Conjola. While his wife sheltered in the basement, Greg fought the 40-metre flames. They survived but their home did not. And Greg's hands were left badly burnt. As we talked, he teared up at the loss of his children's baby photos and he mourned the *smell* of his towels and sheets. But he smiled when he told me several of his wife's hairspray cans were pretty much all that survived. A self-described 'glass half-full kind of guy', he was looking forward to getting all his family and friends together to help rebuild. 'It'll be fun,' he said. But then he turned serious. 'Talk to me again in a year, Mel.'

Two months after the fire ended, ABC Illawarra broadcast from Milton, getting out of the studio to check in on how the community was recovering.

In the local IGA, I overheard a conversation between two blokes near the checkout. 'I've still got that much shit lying around. I thought, fuck it, I'm gonna have a burn-off. Some bastard's gotta be the first to light a match in this town.' Everyone laughed, but it was jarring and a bit uncomfortable.

The shop's owner, Shane Wilson, told me the trauma was still there, just beneath the surface. 'You don't have to ask,' he said. 'You can tell in their eyes. A lot of people have got that bit of angriness. A lot of people won't to this day accept any donations or credit because they're too proud. They want to row their own boat but that has a mental strain and that affects them. We can see that in their eyes.'

Shoalhaven mayor Amanda Findley agreed. 'So many people are putting on a brave face,' she said. 'But inside you know that everything is not OK. There's some big tough nuts giving you stick and you can see that they're broken.'

Amanda Findley's biggest concern is that fear and distrust of the bush will linger. She recalls going into Conjola Park just after New Year's Eve and finding people preparing for the fire's potential return. They were tearing down anything that hadn't burnt – trees, hedges, even rose bushes – and had a large tip truck to take it all away. She said she saw 'dead-set fear in their eyes'. They were cutting down anything combustible, saying 'this bastard's not getting us a second time round'.

The south coast bush is what makes us who we are – it's where we live, where we holiday, or where we grow up and grow old. But after this fire, called Currowan, which circled like a slow-moving shark, and which by the time it was done had burnt 80 per cent of the Shoalhaven local government area, Amanda Findley was not the only one who wondered whether our relationship with the bush would ever be the same.

Melinda James is a journalist and broadcaster based in Wollongong at ABC Illawarra

A Black Horizon

Jonathon Kendall

AFTER DRIVING HALF A DAY TO MALLACOOTA, WE'VE BOARDED a boat to Gabo Island, one of the most beautiful and isolated parts of Victoria. There's hardly any swell or wind. A beautiful day. I'm with my mum, sister and brother-in-law, as well as my wife, Belinda, and our two very excited kids.

Halfway to the island my phone vibrates. It's a text message: 'You need to leave East Gippsland today 29 December for a safer location as fires are likely to impact this area.' There's a link at the bottom to a Victorian government website.

Hang on. What? Everyone needs to get out of East Gippsland? That can't be right. East Gippsland is a big place. Its centre is Bairnsdale, home to 15,000 people. It's also the height of the summer tourist season. There would be more than 100,000 people in the region right now, most of them in coastal areas. Are all those people supposed to evacuate? Where will they all go? I need some more specifics. The message doesn't even say who it's from. If this is real, surely it's overreach.

And as I'm grappling with this, our boat docks at Gabo Island.

Gabo is a place I've heard so much about but never had time to get to until now. A wild island in Bidawal country, it's only 154 hectares and is just three kilometres long and one kilometre at its widest point, shaped like an upside-down comma. It's 14 kilometres east from Mallacoota but because of the curve of the coastline, its northern tail almost whips the beaches of Croajingolong National Park. It sits in the waters of the Cape Howe Marine Park and the name Gabo is most likely an Aboriginal pronunciation of Cape Howe.

The island is run by Parks Victoria and when we get there we're greeted by the lighthouse caretaker, Leo op den Brouw, a salty old seadog who seems to have become a product of this environment. He's extremely knowledgeable, helpful, friendly, and loves the island and its history. He picks us up from the wharf in a trumped-up golf buggy, the only vehicle that's allowed on the island because the landscape is so sensitive. Gabo is home to thousands of penguins and seabirds and their fragile sandy burrows, not to mention seals and the odd cow to keep the kikuyu grass down.

We're staying in the assistant lightkeeper's cottage. It's a historic building but one of those places you immediately feel at home in: large armchairs and couches, big lamps, eight comfy beds, and artwork on the walls from previous guests. It even has its very own library of CDs: kd lang, Tony Bennett, some hard NRG trance and compilation albums from the 90s. The cottage has been a sanctuary from the ocean's howling gales for more than a hundred years, and you can sit on the southeast-facing verandah and watch the weather come in.

We are so busy exploring that first day I don't really give the text message all that much more thought – plus I don't seem to have mobile reception. I ask Leo about the threat and he promises to keep us updated if anything breaks out. Right now, an island 14 kilometres from Mallacoota seems like a reasonably safe place to be.

—

The next day Leo gives us a tour of the 167-year-old lighthouse, made of pink granite quarried from the island. The kids really get a kick out of being up so high – 47 metres – and looking down on the seals, ocean and cottages below and out to the horizon.

I still don't have any mobile signal, but the others have got a tiny bit: one bar of reception in a spot near the back door of the house. That night we check the VicEmergency app and see that a fire has started in thick bush near Wingan River, west of Mallacoota. An emergency warning has been issued for Mallacoota. The app tells us that the westerly wind is expected to pick up and the town could be threatened.

Before we go to bed that night Belinda pulls me aside. 'Leo has left the tractor out of the shed and laid a fire hose around the outside,' she says. 'Do you reckon he's worried about embers making it here?'

'I'm sure he's just being cautious,' I say so we can get some sleep.

But when I get up in the night to go to the toilet I look across to the mainland and see a frightening orange glow around Mallacoota. It's not looking good.

We wake early the next day, New Year's Eve, and the westerly is howling. It feels unreal. By 8 am there's a huge black cloud over the mainland and the wind is coming straight from the fire ground towards us. We've all been in bushfire situations before, so we know what it's like when the sky goes dark, but we all agree it is a touch more disconcerting when you're on an island with young kids. At least I can see one patch of blue sky to the south. Burnt leaves are starting to land on the island. It's too windy to be outside so we're all cooped up in the cottage. By 8.15 am the patch of blue has disappeared; the sky is pink and orange and the black cloud seems to be steaming towards us from the mainland.

By 10 am it feels like it's 10 pm. It's pitch-black outside and the kids are starting to get spooked. I've spent hours inventing games with them inside and now I'm in Leo's office. I've decided to record an interview with him each day we're on the island so that I can file to ABC Gippsland. He's just submitted the latest weather observations to the Bureau of Meteorology, all part of his job. He reckons living on the island is quite slow until it's suddenly not. 'As long as we don't get any burning embers we'll just cruise along and see what happens,' he says.

When he's not on the island, Leo lives on one of the streets in Mallacoota that borders the bush and it looks like it will be hit pretty hard.

'There are friends there; young families live across the road,' he says. 'I'm quite concerned for some of them. I hope they've all had some success. What really worries me is if their houses will survive and how they're faring mentally and physically.'

We are supposed to be getting the boat back to Mallacoota today and heading home but that clearly isn't happening. Leo's daughter Cass and her kids have joined us on Gabo, evacuating Mallacoota before the fire hits. We have been told we can stay on the island until the food runs out and it's safe to get off, and we've been in touch with Parks Victoria and the police, who are keeping track of us in the incident control centre in Bairnsdale. They're telling us to stay put until we can be evacuated.

We've moved the old stereo to a part of the house that can get a skerrick of reception to pick up ABC Gippsland and we're listening to it a fair bit. The situation in Mallacoota sounds pretty bad. We know that houses have been destroyed. Four thousand tourists are sheltering on the beach waiting for the fire to come. Gas bottles are in the shallows so they don't explode.

Jonathon Kendall filming at Bruthen, Victoria. (Peter Somerville/ABC)

Jonathon Kendall's family running for their flight off Gabo Island.
(Jonathon Kendall)

Families with kids are out in boats, floating around so they can stay safe. And locals are dealing with the terrible destruction of a ravenous fire.

It doesn't feel like New Year's Eve. I have one beer and try not to eat too much in case we need to ration food.

On New Year's Day the guilt hits. We have a dilemma. Leo is the State Emergency Service (SES) controller for Mallacoota and is a pretty important community leader. He needs to get off the island to be with his community but his boss has told him to stay and babysit us. We could go with him but we're not keen on taking our chances in Mallacoota with limited supplies and the road closed.

Belinda and I alternate between keeping the kids busy and having meetings to discuss if we should be trying to get off the island so that Leo can go home. But what will we find when we get to Mallacoota? Our car was parked next to tea trees so it has probably burnt – and even if it has survived and manages to start, the Princes Highway home is closed.

We are cooped up inside because of the smoke. It's extremely thick and only a few moments outside leaves our clothes smelling like we've been at a bonfire. We can see a large grey navy vessel over at Mallacoota and we reckon it's HMAS *Choules.* There's a suggestion they might send a chopper to fly us off the island. I almost scoff at the thought and actually make a bet with my mum that it won't happen. We've been told a boat is coming this afternoon and will be taking Leo's daughter and her kids back to Mallacoota tomorrow. I reckon we should get on it too. But my sister, my mum and Belinda disagree.

The next day is more of the same. We're struggling to keep the kids contained inside but the smoke is so thick we don't want to let them out. Burnt leaves continue to land on the island. After spending a bit too long in doona cubbies and reading too many books, the kids burst out the back door and we have running races on the kikuyu grass in the thick smoke.

We have decided to stay. Supplies are getting low but Leo brings us a second box of food, including a jumbo jar of peanut butter and some self-raising flour. In between visits to the reception spot at the back door to check her phone, my mum makes us scones and we top them off with our newly acquired peanut butter. Cass generously brings round a box of fresh food for us before she leaves, including olives, mangoes, chicken, snow peas from her garden and sourdough bread.

That night we invite Leo over for a chicken stir-fry dinner made from the ingredients Cass has given us. After taking a few mouthfuls he tells us he'll duck back to the caretaker's cottage to get some beer. He returns with four beers and his phone. 'You better down this beer pretty quickly because a chopper is coming to get you at 6 o'clock,' he says, and there are a few hoots of joy before we realise we only have 20 minutes to pack everything up and get the kids ready for a helicopter ride.

The Taipan chopper from HMAS *Choules* touches down on the island with military precision. Its crew is friendly and help us put on helmets, ear plugs and ear muffs, which our two-year-old hates and rips off.

As we're getting the gear on, I ask one of the crew why we get to be evacuated before the thousands of tourists and residents on the beach at Mallacoota. He says they were heading to Bairnsdale to refuel anyway. Our four-year-old goes quiet in the chopper and looks scared. The two-year-old is now bawling. But we are so grateful to be leaving and to everyone who is making it possible.

This is part of a massive military response. We find out later the chopper crews were working from dusk to dawn, in hot and smoky conditions, to get vital supplies in and evacuees out. Over the next few days HMAS *Choules* transports thousands of holidaymakers and their pets to Hastings south of Melbourne. Its crew had been recalled from their holiday break on New Year's Eve to work on Operation Bushfire Assist. And then there's the Australian army reservists who work for a month to clear and re-open the Princes Highway, assisted by troops from neighbouring countries, including Indonesia, Fiji and Papua New Guinea. It will be only the third time the PNG Defence Force has ever been deployed overseas and is its largest deployment ever. Three Royal New Zealand Air Force helicopters and their crew are also sent over the ditch to help.

After one day resting, I go straight into emergency broadcasting, getting vital information to communities. Then comes the recovery. And making sure locals aren't forgotten in the fallout of a national emergency. Months later, I go back to Mallacoota and stand in the devastated and eerily quiet bush. I broadcast from the town and chat with locals about the fires and their hopes for the future. I see some of the 120 homes that were destroyed. Belinda and I collect our car from the boat ramp, complete with plastic that melted when the tea trees just metres away went up in flames.

The recovery from this will take years. As for Gabo, we haven't yet been back there. But we will. Hopefully for a more relaxing stay.

Jonathon Kendall is an ABC journalist and presenter

Escape from the Flames

Jade Macmillan

THERE IS A LOT WE USUALLY TAKE FOR GRANTED IN AUSTRALIA. Clean air, for example. Safe drinking water, a tank full of petrol, and mobile phones connecting us to the world. The spread of coronavirus has caused a sense of emergency on a scale most of us have never experienced before. But in bushfire-affected parts of the country, it feels all too familiar.

Driving to the New South Wales south coast from Canberra on New Year's Eve, my ABC colleagues and I felt nervous. Mild anxiety before a big assignment is normal, the adrenaline helping to push you through long days and the pressures of filing. But as we passed under dark then bright orange clouds near Cooma, we wondered what we were headed towards. Road closures forced us to find a back route, obsessively checking the RFS Fires Near Me app and Live Traffic website along the way to choose the safest option. Technology provides a level of comfort, the reassurance that the information we need is at our fingertips. Until it fails.

Early on New Year's Day we made our way to the coastal community of Bermagui, where thousands of people had evacuated to the local surf club or hurriedly set up camp on grassed areas nearby. Little to no phone signal meant we couldn't file live TV reports as we'd planned. It was a mild inconvenience compared to the impact on residents.

Richelle Jackson and her three young boys had escaped to the coast in the early hours of the morning the day before from their dairy farm at Coolagolite, near the badly hit town of Cobargo. 'The boys and I stayed for a period until the fire reached our farm and the ferocity of it was pretty huge, just the noise and the heat that came before it,' she told us. 'It was coming up the hill and we were bunkering in the dairy. The boys were under woollen blankets and I was out there trying to just wet things down. And I'm usually pretty resilient but it was the kind of sound that made you go really weak at the knees.'

Richelle's husband had stayed at the property to try to protect their dairy herd and the communications breakdown meant she couldn't get through to him. 'I was relieved to get the boys out of there but it was scary leaving your husband behind,' she said.

Mobile phone outages weren't confined to Bermagui. Further north at Narooma, we noticed a group of people lining up on the side of the road, waiting to use one of the only forms of communication left – a payphone. Many of them were tourists, trying to reassure panicked family back home that they were OK. Others wanted to check on friends around the region. 'A bit of a throwback,' a teenage girl remarked, gesturing to the payphone, but one she was thankful for.

Lines started becoming a common sight as the crisis wore on. The first time we saw people queuing for groceries was in Narooma on New Year's Day. The power was out but the local IGA borrowed a generator from another shop nearby and opened up to shoppers, who used the torches on their mobile phones to browse the dark aisles. 'There are people here who don't have anything, they've been evacuated and they've come with nothing,' the owner said.

Major road closures meant that even the large supermarkets had difficulty keeping their shelves stocked. Bags of ice became a rare commodity and bottled water got harder to find. Some stores ran out of baked beans and tinned spaghetti. Staff guarded the front entrance, letting in small groups at a time. They explained that not all of their colleagues could come to work because they'd lost their homes, and those who were there were doing the best they could. I never once saw the type of panic buying or aggression caused by Covid-19.

We'd barely begun to understand the scale of the damage caused on New Year's Eve when visitors to the area were given an unprecedented warning. Conditions were forecast to worsen again that weekend, prompting the RFS to declare a massive

Queuing for a public phone, Narooma, NSW. (Jade Macmillan)

Residents being briefed at the Narooma evacuation centre. (Jade Macmillan)

'tourist leave zone' all the way from south of Nowra to the Victorian border.

With road closures still in place and limited fuel supplies, moving thousands of people in just a couple of days wasn't easy. Power outages prevented some petrol stations from opening and the ones that could had long lines of motorists waiting to fill up before they could get out. Traffic jams formed in small country towns, and major highways became clogged with cars, trucks and caravans as people spent hours taking the long way around to avoid areas still burning.

Once the tourists had gone, many locals felt some sense of relief. Their communities were still under extreme threat but at least they could now focus all of their attention on each other and their preparations. Like so many others had already done, the worst-case scenario for some involved evacuating to the beach.

Larry Vogelnest was one of hundreds of people who had been forced onto the sand at Malua Bay on New Year's Eve. He had evacuated from nearby Rosedale with his partner and her 11-year-old son as the fire got closer.

'You could feel the heat and the wind coming over,' he said. 'There must have been about a thousand people there, all crammed on the beach, and it was just frightening, absolutely frightening. We knew as adults that we were probably going to be fine. But I think for the kids, it was something they couldn't comprehend, they just thought they were going to die.'

As the predicted catastrophic days grew closer, people in the town of Moruya were considering their options. An evacuation centre was up and running but long-time resident Ryan Gallagher was also preparing for the possibility of heading to the river instead.

We met on the jetty near his house and watched waterbombers swooping down to the water to re-fill. When I asked what his evacuation plan was, he said, 'Possibly come right where I am. Stand by the river, ready to jump in if I need to. I only live just up the road along the riverbank so I can make my way to here pretty quickly.'

Ryan described the sense of nervousness felt across the community. 'There's a fire rip-roaring in that's meant to take us out,' he said. 'You can kind of feel that tentative angst in the air. You know it's coming and you prepare the best you can.'

Ahead of the worsening conditions we headed to Narooma, one of the towns feared to be most at risk. An indoor sports stadium was serving as the official evacuation centre and while the media was kept out for privacy reasons, local shire councillor and volunteer Lindsay Brown recalls there being hundreds of people inside as well as 'probably 60 dogs and cats and a bird'.

'There were people who had brought their own bedding, some people had brought mattresses, fold-up beds, others had just brought blankets,' he said. 'We had ladies and gentlemen who came in their walkers and sat in their walkers. They slept in a seated position, they couldn't get down onto the ground.'

Local businesses and charities helped to keep the centre stocked with supplies while evacuees were offered medical and mental health support. 'In Narooma you couldn't see where the fire had been, but you saw the glow, you saw the threat,' Lindsay said. 'You knew it was coming, but you didn't know when. Some people told me that they in some ways hoped the fire would come through and burn their house down because at least then we'd know. Evacuating multiple times, the stress in that is just incredible.'

Rather than going to the evacuation centre, many in Narooma had set up camp at the edge of the local inlet. Some told us they were from smaller communities nearby where they didn't feel safe. They had tents, camping chairs and cooking gear, and their kids played in the shallow water. If it wasn't for the smoky skies and the nervous atmosphere, it might have seemed like a normal summer holiday spot. But people were prepared for the worst and if the situation got too dangerous, they planned to get into the water.

In town, residents did what they could to try to safeguard their homes. The RFS asked those defending their properties to leave their yellow-lid recycling bins out the front so firefighters would know who had stayed behind. A large fishing boat stocked with food and water invited on board elderly people and those with children, in case they needed to head out to sea. Hundreds packed into the evacuation centre car park each day for the latest briefings from officials standing on the back of a ute with a microphone. And then they waited.

On Saturday afternoon, 4 January, the sky turned orange before becoming dark much earlier than normal. Thick ash, like the stuff that had rained down on Bega earlier in the day, started falling, forcing people on the water's edge into their cars. Thankfully, though, the night didn't bring the devastation that had been feared. Narooma was spared for the time being.

Australia's Black Summer wasn't yet over and residents on the south coast would endure more heartache before the crisis ended. But even when the emergency passed, it would still be a long time before life returned to any sense of normality.

—

On the morning of New Year's Eve, Maddy Barry's patisserie in Bermagui was full of people who had just been evacuated from towns nearby.

'You'd say, "How are you, guys?" and they'd just look at us so blank and say, "I don't think we have a house any more,"' she said. 'And for some people it was true and for some people they didn't find out for days afterwards if they did or didn't.'

Maddy gave away free food and coffee and put a donation bucket for the local RFS on the counter. By the time she had to close the shop – when the fire threat intensified later that morning – she says more than $2000 had been raised.

Patisserie owner Maddy Barry and her kids in Canberra. (Jade Macmillan)

A week later, I caught up with Maddy in Canberra where she and her young family were staying with relatives while they waited for the danger to pass and for Bermagui's essential services to be restored.

Her business was still closed, most of its perishable stock had been lost and the usually busy summer trading period had been brought to an abrupt end. But work wasn't her only concern.

'You never want to have that conversation with your four-year-old about why it's not safe to go home,' she said. 'It's heartbreaking.'

Months later, she's still mindful of the impact the fires had on her two small children, Willow and Eli.

'When we were up there [in Canberra] I'd bought them some toys from Questacon and [later] one of them broke and so Willow asked if she could have another one. And I said, "Yeah, next time we go to Canberra we'll see if they still sell them," and she asked, "Next time we go to Canberra like next time our house is going to burn down?"'

Through the most challenging times, small acts of kindness have inspired hope. When Maddy's business eventually re-opened, a seven-year-old girl celebrating her birthday asked her mum to donate the cost of a cake so the patisserie could make one for someone who deserved it. The recipient ended up being a long-time RFS volunteer who had recently become a grandmother. Cash has also been donated with the request that coffees for strangers are shouted until it runs out.

It's that sense of community that Maddy was hoping would continue when Covid-19 first emerged. While her business has taken another hit, when we last spoke she felt lucky not to have been as badly affected by the pandemic as many others around the country.

She says people in her area are still focused on trying to recover from the fires.

'Countless customers are still living in caravans or short-term rentals or have made the decision to sell their land and move into town,' she said. 'There are people who are only just taking their first steps towards rebuild or renewal, whatever that is for them.'

Jade Macmillan is a political reporter in the ABC's Parliament House Bureau in Canberra

Displaced

Matthew Doran

The school gymnasium was hot and humid, with people milling around, chatting and passing the time, likely still in shock at what had happened less than 24 hours earlier. Helena Pluim sat in the middle of it all with her two dogs, Boots and Ted. One dog rested on her lap, the other by her feet. Despite the hubbub around her, she stared off into the distance, expressionless.

I asked her the obvious question: 'How are you?'

'I'm just desperate to find out about my daughter,' she said as she burst into tears.

You feel like such a jerk when you ask a question that prompts a reaction like that.

There'd been little to celebrate on New Year's Eve in the Upper Murray Valley, east of Wodonga in northern Victoria. Rather than coming together to mark the year that was, the community had come together to fight a ferocious blaze.

The town of Corryong was at the centre of the inferno. Flames had licked at its edges, razing a few buildings. But, surprisingly, much of the town had been spared. Neighbouring towns such as Cudgewa hadn't been so lucky, with dozens of homes destroyed. The fire was still raging to the south and east of Corryong when ABC cameraman Steve Opie and I arrived on New Year's Day.

I'd been enjoying something of a summer break at home in Adelaide with my family when I got a call from my boss in Canberra on New Year's Eve, asking whether I could jump on a flight to Melbourne that night. At six o'clock the following morning, Steve and I hit the road, heading north to Corryong – all the while listening to the emergency warnings being played over ABC Radio. The broadcast provided valuable information on what the fire was doing, but also a crash course in the various town names in the region. Mispronunciations on air are a cardinal sin at the best of times, let alone during an emergency.

Rolling into Tallangatta, west of Corryong, there was a flurry of activity. Fire trucks from across Victoria and over the other side of the Murray in New South Wales lined the main street. Weary crews were pouring out of the local bakery, which had been running a 24-hour operation since the emergency began. The production line making salad rolls was something to behold.

Tallangatta was the main evacuation hub for the entire valley and the command post for the firefighting efforts; it was around an hour's drive from where the front had ringed Corryong a few hours earlier.

The valley itself had been locked down by Victoria Police. No one was allowed into the area, with the fire behaviour deemed too erratic to safely allow access. But after a few hours of negotiation, Steve and I managed to get a spot in a convoy of emergency services vehicles heading to Corryong with supplies.

The rolling fields were covered in grey smoke, as far as the eye could see. If it wasn't for the smell, you'd be forgiven for thinking it was just a foggy winter's day. The convoy travelled quite slowly, snaking its way around fallen trees and downed power lines. Then Corryong appeared on the horizon and it became clear why we had seen almost no other vehicles coming in the opposite direction. Police had stopped locals from leaving the town, the roads considered too dangerous.

Dozens and dozens of cars lined the road outside the school, where a community meeting was just wrapping up in the gym. That's where we met Helena Pluim. She'd moved from Melbourne to Corryong a few years prior, to be closer to her daughter, who lived in the nearby New South Wales town of Tooma. Helena's house was fine, but she'd packed up her belongings and her two dogs, evacuating to the school gym as a precaution. With power supplies down and phone lines damaged in the fire, her sole concern was her daughter.

'I got on to her last night, and the fires were coming around, and that's the last I heard from her,' she told me, wiping away tears.

The advice to the locals in Corryong was, for the moment, that they had the option of staying in the town or evacuating under police escort.

'I'm 61 years old, and I can't make up my mind,' Helena said. 'I want my daughter. I want to make sure she's alright.'

There's a certain ghoulishness in shoving a microphone and a camera in someone's face when they're experiencing such fear. But over the summer I noticed time and time again how willing people were to share their stories. They were tired and scared. Some had already lost their homes. Others didn't know if theirs were still standing. But the moment we arrived, ABC microphone in hand, they'd open up. Or they'd at least dob in a mate to talk to us instead.

Thanking Helena, and making sure to give Ted and Boots plenty of attention before leaving, I was drawn to the volunteers working in the hall. Each had a role and they were getting on with their work. No fuss, no bother. One woman was wandering around the hall, handing out hot cups of tea in polystyrene cups. Another was restocking a table where people could make ham, lettuce and cheese rolls. They were ably supported by a crew working in a small room off to the side, doing food preparation under the glow of a portable workshop lamp. Volunteers weren't too keen on us looking in there, worried the set-up wouldn't

The road into Corryong, Victoria. (Matthew Doran)

Helena Pluim in the Corryong school gymnasium. (Matthew Doran)

meet the usual health and safety standards. Somehow, I didn't think they were going to get slapped with a warning notice, not at a time like this.

Fred and Ruth Coulston were benefitting from the hospitality, sitting outside with a cup of tea.

Fred, nearly 90, was born in Corryong and had lived there his whole life. But he and Ruth were reluctantly preparing to evacuate the area. 'I would elect to stay here, but they won't let me,' Fred said, smiling.

Fred had seen many fires before, but nothing this ferocious. He was a student at the local school during a blaze in 1939, and was on the front line fighting another fire in 1952. Back in the 1930s, wet hessian sacks and uprooted bushes were used to extinguish blazes, rather than trucks, helicopters and water bombers.

When I asked what they'd be doing once they left town, Fred deferred to his wife for more details. I got the feeling he often let Ruth do the talking. The pair were going to stay with family in one of the larger towns nearby, Ruth told me, outside of the immediate danger zone. 'It's hard, very hard to learn that you have to leave,' she said, 'but you learn that you must care for yourself.'

The dogs sheltering with their owners at the Corryong school were in their element. So many new friends and so many pats to be had. Ten-year-old Scarlet Leone was traipsing after one of the dogs when she tapped me on the arm. Her family were from Narooma, on the New South Wales south coast, and had fled the fires there, seeking safety in their holiday home in the Upper Murray Valley.

'We came here to escape the fires, which as you can see didn't turn out that well,' Scarlet said matter-of-factly. As soon as they could, Scarlet, her parents and their dog would be heading to Melbourne.

Evacuation centres like this one at Corryong became a feature of many communities throughout the devastating summer, providing much-needed respite for people fleeing the flames. Many came through the doors with little but the clothes on their back and whatever they could bundle into their cars at the last minute. They were weary, hungry and needing somewhere to rest their heads – even if it was just for a few minutes or a few hours.

They were all met with friendly faces and comforting food. None of the volunteers were brushing over the fact it was an emergency. They weren't trying to avoid the subject or pretend it wasn't something to worry about. Rather, they were trying to keep people upright, saving sanity in a time of crisis. People would come and go, as needed. Some evacuated from their homes over and over again, as the unpredictable fires changed direction over and over again. The doors were always open, and the welcome always there.

Many evacuation centres became hubs of the community. The point where information about the emergency was delivered by police and fire authorities. The outlet for supplies trucked in to be handed out to people who couldn't make it to the local shop. The first point of contact for people needing medical treatment, with St John's Ambulance volunteers keeping a vigil, triaging those who needed more support in larger towns or cities.

On 2 January, Helena Pluim messaged me and the relief in her text was palpable. She'd been able to get in contact with her daughter after emergency phone services had been restored to the valley. 'I'm so emotional,' she wrote. 'We are about to head off, I hate leaving her.'

Helena had managed to make up her mind, deciding it was best to evacuate from the valley because conditions were expected to take a turn for the worse in coming days. Police were preparing evacuation orders for much of the valley, and she had joined a convoy of residents on their slow retreat from the place they called home. Her daughter, however, was staying on her farm with her partner to look after their horses.

'I am worried sick with her choice,' Helena said. 'I'm not sure where I am going, as my head is in a whirlwind, but I slept like a log last night.'

Helena and I exchanged a steady stream of messages back and forth over the next few hours. She sent photos of the convoy, and of her daughter and her precious horses. Helena told me she had struck up a conversation with a woman also waiting to leave, and they'd swapped stories of what they'd been through and, most importantly, what they were looking forward to once the crisis was over.

Steve and I were back in Tallangatta at this point, and I told Helena we'd be staying in the region to report on the fires for at least a few more days – until our own reinforcements came. Before signing off, she had one last thing to offer, in case we got stuck over the next few days. 'If you go to Corryong and need a place to stay, let me know,' she said. 'There are two double beds, plenty of linen. I've turned the power off at the box – you just need to turn it on.'

Matthew Doran is a political reporter in the ABC's Parliament House bureau in Canberra

Escape to the Jetty

Stacey Lee

It's a Thursday. Thursday, 9 January, to be exact. But days and dates mean little now. Time is elusive under these circumstances.

I have been working on Kangaroo Island with my colleague camera operator Trent Murphy for a number of days now, reporting on a relentless blaze that has been burning for 20 days straight. It's already destroyed half of the island, ordinarily known for its pristine coastline and stunning national parks.

We're tired.

But we're nowhere near as exhausted as the locals and the selfless fire crews.

Hundreds of Kangaroo Islanders on the western side of the island are today packing up their belongings and fleeing to safer ground in the east. We've spent the day interviewing them. For many, this is the second or third time this summer they've had to do this: it's a well-oiled machine, but that doesn't make it any easier to leave their house or business to the mercy of the fires. Hard work and memories are being left behind, potentially turning to ashes before the day is out.

Fire crews tell us tonight will be 'the big one'. A wind change is predicted that will push the fire east towards the so-far untouched, more-populated part of Kangaroo Island. There will be strong wind gusts to fan the flames. To fan disaster.

Trent and I have sent today's story back to the ABC's Adelaide office for the 7 pm news. We set up for live crosses at the airport, 14 kilometres east of Kingscote, the largest town on the island. The Country Fire Service (CFS) and the army are based here, and I ask the CFS boss to confirm the current situation, to ensure my reporting is up to date for the live cross. He points up at a cloud and tells me that it is their main concern. It's a pyrocumulonimbus cloud. They're the dangerous ones. They can create their own weather patterns. Anyone who's ever worked on a fire ground will tell you that unpredictable and changing weather patterns are one of the biggest problems they face. It's not looking good.

Then we notice the defence personnel packing up their tents and leaving the airport. Dozens of them had been camping in a grassy paddock alongside the runway for days, while they helped the fire crews. I ask them where they're going and they tell me that, like the residents we've been following all day, they are heading east to Kingscote. The army has just been told that the airport is under threat. The very place housing the heroes working tirelessly to save lives and homes is now in the fire's devastating path.

It's going to be a long night.

Trent and I finish crossing live into the Adelaide, Sydney and national news bulletins and head back to Kingscote for our nightly debrief with our colleagues who've been working with us on the island over the past few days. We have dinner around 9 pm, discuss the day and head back to the two-bedroom apartment we're sharing. We each take showers and lay out our fire gear so it can air overnight before we have to put it on again tomorrow. We've been wearing the heavy fire boots, pants and jacket for days, so by now the smell of smoke is embedded not just in the fabric but in my hair too. No matter how much shampoo I use, the ashy smell lingers. I usually wear contact lenses but my eyes are so irritated by the hazy air on the island that I've had to fish out my back-up pair of glasses from the bottom of my handbag. We turn the TV on and watch the news to catch up on what has happened throughout the day. Not much else it seems: it's wall-to-wall fire coverage from almost every Australian state.

Around midnight, we decide it's time for bed so we head into our separate rooms. As on previous nights, I can hear the CFS scanner still switched on in Trent's room. He knows better than to turn it off. In hindsight, I don't think he ever had any intention of sleeping. As well as being a full-time camera operator with the ABC in Adelaide, Trent is also a CFS volunteer. Over the past few days, his knowledge of fire grounds has been crucial. Even though the ABC has very strict protocols in place for heading into a fire ground, it can sometimes be daunting to drive into a dangerous situation when you see most other people driving away from it, escaping to safer areas. But with Trent as my work partner I have felt comfortable, confident and safe.

I have barely fallen asleep when Trent is opening my bedroom door and demanding that we leave. Now. The fire is approaching Kingscote and the whole town is under threat. I check the time: 1.30 am. Things have changed so much in just an hour and a half.

I quickly pull on my fire gear, which still reeks of smoke, grab my phone and glasses, and we jump in the car. We head west, towards the fire, aiming to get vision of it if we can. We've been told by our Adelaide-based boss not to go too far, to stay safe, to only get what we need to tell the story and then get to safer ground. But we can't even get close. Police roadblocks are in place, keeping everyone in Kingscote.

Usually in this part of the world, thousands of bright, flickering stars fill the evening sky. Not tonight. Tonight, there's a menacing orange glow overtaking the dark. It's an unsettling sight.

Since we can't get any closer to the front, Trent and I reassess and agree we should head back into town to see how people are coping. But we can't find anyone. Lights are off in houses, and roads are empty. Is everyone asleep in bed, unaware that the fire is on their doorstep? Surely not.

We decide to head to the jetty.

It's packed. It looks as if everyone on the island has gathered there. Cars are lined up for kilometres. I've never seen anything like it. They're all parking each other in; it's clear no one's going anywhere anytime soon. We pull over where we can find a spot and walk about a kilometre down to the jetty. The air is tense, yet the mood is calm. Some people are outside their cars talking and drinking with family, others are inside comforting their children. A rare few are sleeping, or trying to at least.

Trent and I recognise about a dozen people. Some we'd interviewed a couple of days ago, others we'd helped evacuate earlier today. One woman I remember from a Kingscote bar a few nights ago; she had thanked me, and the rest of the ABC, for being on the island and covering their stories.

We approach an older couple. I recognise the woman, but can't place her right now. They're standing arm in arm, alongside their dog, and agree to an interview. I ask them on camera how they're feeling. The woman, Jeanene Ellson, replies in an upbeat voice, 'We're all pretty stressed but we think the safest place to be is near the sea, so that if you have to go in the water, you can.' She says this in such a positive tone that I almost don't register the seriousness of the statement. I don't like guessing people's ages, but I'd say she and her husband are

Camera operator Steve Opie films emergency workers clearing a road at Charleston, SA. (Stacey Lee/ABC)

in their seventies. To think that they are ready to jump in the water is gut-wrenching.

I ask her husband, Peter, how he's feeling. 'I just can't get my head around it,' he replies. 'It's never happened in my whole life on the island, never happened like this.' He seems anxious, and I'm conscious of not adding to the stress that these people are already dealing with, so we stop rolling. I thank them for their time and ask them if there's anything we can do to help. Peter touches my arm, leans in and asks me if they are safe at the jetty. He's not looking directly at me and it's in that moment that I realise he's blind and the dog with him is a guide dog. 'It's just that I can't see,' he explains. 'I am meant to be the one looking after Jeanene, but instead I'm just following and I feel helpless. Please tell me we're safe here?'

I'm lost for words. I think they're in the right place, but these fires have been so unpredictable that anything might happen tonight. I don't want to give him false hope, but I also don't want to worry him even more. I tell him that he's in the safest place he can be and that I haven't seen a fire truck in the town at all, which is a good thing. It means the crews are still fighting the blaze outside of Kingscote and have, so far, stopped it reaching the town.

'Thank you, thank you for that,' he says as he lets go of my arm and searches for his wife's hand to hold. I give them my number in case we can help with anything and then Trent and I leave them.

As soon as I am far enough away that I'm out of sight and earshot I burst into tears. I lose it completely. I'm not usually one to cry, particularly while on the job, but I just can't control it this time. It's such a helpless feeling to witness vulnerable people in an uncontrolled and unpredictable situation. I try to think of anything I can do to help, but short of getting on a fire truck, the best thing I can do is continue to get the public safety warnings out to the community.

I take a breath, wipe my face and we move on. We talk to a few other people and gather interviews and camera vision to be used in the news coverage. Then we head to Kingscote oval, which has been set up as a relief centre. Locals and holidaymakers displaced by the fire have been camping there and sleeping in their cars for some time. As we get in the car to leave the jetty, I remember where I recognise Jeanene from. She's been volunteering her time at the relief centre, making sandwiches for people who have lost their homes and have nothing to eat. Thinking of her selflessness makes me tear up again. No one deserves to be in this situation. Ever.

—

That night, the fire almost reaches the airport. Crews manage to stop it about three kilometres out, but not before it burns through tens of thousands more hectares. Eventually around 210,000 hectares of Kangaroo Island are blackened in the blaze, which will not be officially declared 'controlled' until 21 January, over a month after it started. Two men have died while fighting this fire. Eighty-nine houses have been destroyed, along with almost 300 sheds, farmhouses and other outbuildings. For most, the scale of destruction and loss is immeasurable, and it will take years for the community of Kangaroo Island to rebuild.

Stacey Lee is the state political reporter in the ABC's Adelaide newsroom

HEROES

It surprised me whom I looked to for leadership and whose arms I found comfort in. People I didn't know very well – like Steve Hope, a local café owner – suddenly gave the best hugs in town. He steadily went about his days making free food and coffee, giving people a slice of comfort and normality.

People like Cheryl McCarthy, Bruce McAslan and Lobba from the surf club. The sacrifices they made for their community will be long remembered. People like Tim Holdsworth and his team from the Bermagui RFS. Asked and expected to do the impossible, they worked for weeks straight on little sleep with minimal backup. People like Paul Lazzaro, who sacrificed his own safety to protect key water assets for the council and town. And the many people who worked behind the scenes so that Bermagui didn't burn – the farmers on the edge of town who worked tirelessly with heavy machinery operators, like Bruce Jamieson, to create fire breaks.

But the person who surprised me the most was my partner, Yannis. He never faltered in his duty to his community, and if something needed doing, he was the first to offer his hand. Day after day, when I wanted to selfishly concede to my exhaustion, he pushed me to keep going. He provided a calmness and support to me that I honestly didn't know he was capable of. And it brought us immeasurably closer – despite the nightmare we were living through.

These people – these heroes – gave us a glimmer of hope in our darkest of days. A million thank yous will never be enough.

Claire Wheaton

The Bermagui community gathers for a briefing in the lead-up to the next catastrophic fire day. (Matt Roberts/ABC)

Wollemi National Park, NSW. (Mridula Amin/ABC)

The Black Ops Brigade

Matthew Doran

If you were to think of a quintessential country pub, the Wollombi Tavern would fit the bill. It has a high front bar, made of timber worn smooth by those who've propped it up over the years, and a kitchen out the back serving wholesome, filling food. The friendly locals pulling beers know everyone's name and their usual tipple of choice.

But there's a curious white line running along the length of the outside wall. It isn't a quirk of the wood panelling encasing the pub – it has been deliberately traced.

'It's the level where the water came up to in the last big flood,' one local told me, as he watched me pondering the marking.

Like the majority of rural and regional communities across Australia, Wollombi and neighbouring hamlets clinging to the edge of the Yengo National Park, around 130 kilometres north of Sydney, are at the mercy of the elements. From floods to fires, they've copped it on plenty of occasions before. And they've recovered plenty of times too.

After a long day on the road, I was nursing a pint out the front of the tavern with cameraman Michael Clements, waiting for a schnitzel and chips to satisfy my considerable hunger.

It was early December 2019 and thick smoke hung in the air. People from the town and its surrounds were still enjoying the hospitality of their local, spilling out onto the street, but the mood was one of fatigue.

On 6 December, three fires – Gospers Mountain, Little L Complex and Paddock Run – had joined together into what was being dubbed a 'mega-fire'. It stretched from Wollombi to just north of Sydney's outer reaches, and had scorched an area larger than the city's greater metropolitan area. By the time it was brought under control, months after I was there, about a million hectares had been scorched.

It was a sustained attack, threatening lives and property, and the community was drawing on all of its reserves. And relying on a special band of brave locals. When the RFS couldn't reach certain places because their resources were at capacity, these locals were putting themselves in the line of fire, and, anecdotally, without their selfless work many more people would today be without homes and livelihoods.

Collectively, they were called the 'Black Ops'. But they had a few names for themselves. The Renegade Brigade was one, in tribute to the fact they were effectively going against the advice of authorities in what they were doing. The Aldi Strike Force was another – 'twice the value for half the cost' was their motto. Then there were the Mosquitos, buzzing in as the threat flared up and buzzing out once the danger had abated.

People at the tavern were muttering that this fire seemed different from previous ones. Then, all of a sudden, there was a flurry of activity. Phones started pinging with messages. The owners of about half a dozen utes, trucks and SUVs dropped what they were doing and hopped into their vehicles, tearing off down the highway. They had large water tanks strapped to their trays and trailers, and hoses coiled up alongside shovels, hessian sacks and chainsaws.

The Little L fire had changed direction. The Black Ops were taking matters into their own hands.

The next day, Michael and I went as usual to the local RFS station to check in with the local firies – to get a sense of the lay of the land and, most importantly, where we needed to avoid. My phone rang. On the other end of the line was Fiona Migan, a Wollombi local. It turned out that an ABC studio director in our Ultimo headquarters in Sydney was from the Wollombi area and had put my phone number into a community-wide WhatsApp group chat. Fiona saw it and decided to invite us to her home. Not immediately, though. 'Give me a few hours,' she said. 'My husband has been up all night – I want to let him sleep a bit.'

Michael and I spent a bit of time talking to people around town before setting off. As we came around a sweeping bend on the Great North Road, Fiona's modest timber-and-tin home appeared in the distance, perched at the bottom of a hill in an area called Paynes Crossing.

Fiona and a few of her friends were sitting out the front, passing around a bag of fresh grapes and enjoying some cool water. Her husband, Darren Philip, was tinkering away on a car nearby. To say this group of Black Ops looked spent would be an understatement. But they had smiles on their faces and were sharing a few jokes.

'If you don't laugh, you cry,' one quipped.

As if battling a fire wasn't hard enough, the way this mega-fire was behaving made matters all the more concerning. Other than a few flare-ups in the days before we got into town, it seemed the most ferocious activity happened at night. For most of the day, the tall ridge lines marking the edge of the Yengo National Park were shrouded in thick smoke. At night the winds picked up and the veil hiding the bright orange line of fire would be whipped away. Fingers of flame would creep down the hill, teasing and taunting the people living below. Add to that the limited phone reception and there was a real sense of isolation – remarkable, considering we were less than two hours' drive from Sydney.

'We're literally waiting for the fire to descend from the ridge,' Fiona said. 'And it's quite fatiguing, because you think,

Black Ops members Fiona Migan, above, and Darren Philip, below.
(Matthew Doran)

OK, it's on, and you get all your crew around and they're ready and then it doesn't come down. This is a pretty extreme situation. It's not just one bushfire – we're looking at several fires that are coming in and sandwiching our village.'

The entire group was keen to stress that none of them were critical of the RFS. They knew the firefighters were doing their best and that their resources were stretched. Given the poor communications in the district, the RFS sometimes had to pull out of areas that were deemed too dangerous, when even their radios were struggling to work.

'The RFS are pulling amazing jobs, they're doing everything they can. But there's also just amazing community members doing everything they can,' Fiona said.

Darren joined us on the front porch, his friendly pooch Pippin following closely at his heels. He'd lived in the area for many years and said this year's fire was similar to what he'd seen back in 1994, when fires ravaged New South Wales, destroying 225 homes and 800,000 hectares of bushland.

He told us there were at least 30 vehicles in the area, kitted out and ready to race to the fire front when it all kicked off. His own SUV pulled a trailer with a 1000-litre water tank on the back, which he filled up from nearby dams.

'We make sure everyone's looked after, everyone's got care, everyone's resting – that's the main thing,' he told me, as he stroked his thick beard and sipped a strong tea. Protecting homes and livelihoods is important, he said, 'but our tribe, our community's safety, is the most important. You can always rebuild a house. The bush telegraph, word of mouth, gets around and we know where everyone is and whose place is doing what and make sure everyone's safe.'

Over the years Darren has lived in the Wollombi region, it has become more and more popular as a spot for people in the city to flee to on weekends, with many Sydneysiders buying property as rural escapes. This popularity has changed the face of the community, Darren said, and many properties weren't ready for the kind of emergency they were currently facing; some people hadn't done simple things like clearing their gutters or cutting back trees that were overhanging houses.

But some had committed full time and were ready. Even so, they sometimes had to call on the resources of the Black Ops as the summertime inferno bore down.

Another Black Ops member, Jed Duffy, had moved to the area a year earlier, and lived up the road from Fiona and Darren at Stockyard Creek. He took Michael and me to his home, built on the edge of a large clearing, surrounded by steep, dense scrub. The serenity of Jed's slice of paradise was exceptional, broken only by the occasional helicopter flying overhead scouting the fire front. In other circumstances, it would've been the perfect place to escape to.

'Life in Sydney was getting a bit busy, and I fancied a slower pace in life,' Jed told us in his lilting Irish accent.

The peace and quiet of Stockyard Creek may have delivered exactly what the former psychotherapist wanted. For a while. But it had all been turned on its head in December 2019. Jed found himself without the support of firefighters – their radios failing them – as the blaze crept ever closer to his home.

It took three days for the flames to arrive, hitting a few other houses deeper in the valley than his own. The sky turned dark, the smoke became all the more acrid. A red glow replaced the usual sparkling blue sky.

'A crew of people I hardly know from a bar of soap – neighbours – they all just rocked up and started to make sure we had the property prepped,' Jed recounted. 'This group of amazing people kind of stuck around, and when the fire came through they helped guide it around the property, kept everything safe, and I've got somewhere to live as a result.'

Jed hadn't slept properly for days if not weeks, but he was relieved he still had a roof over his head. Saved by the Black Ops, he kitted out his white van with equipment so he too could join their ranks.

'I fully just want to be able to give back to the community in the same way that it served me,' he said. 'My van is loaded, I'm available wherever I can get to. I've got a couple of friends – the fire is slowly approaching their place, and we're set up ready for the fire to come in so we can defend. The relationships that we're building, that's the best defence we have against this fire.'

There was something Fiona, Darren, Jed and their friends didn't expressly say, but it was easy to pick up on: beyond the fatigue of dealing with the current crisis, there was a deep worry there was no end in sight. It was still only early December and fires were raging in pockets up and down the east coast.

And they were right. It did get worse. Much worse.

There's often a stereotypical view of country towns that everyone knows one another, and that people look out for one another. I'll admit that as a city dweller, born and bred, it is a slightly foreign concept. I'd struggle to name more than two or three of the people in my childhood street, let alone the apartment building I now live in.

But beyond having a natter at the post office or the supermarket, the people of Wollombi were putting their lives on the line to help each other. They were working hard to keep their neighbours' morale up and their homes standing. And not thinking twice about pitching in and helping out.

It was totally understandable why they'd want to protect their own homes, and those of their friends – but they were also showing up in the driveways of people who were total strangers.

'This is the Wollombi spirit,' Fiona told me, with a smile on her face. 'This is how we roll.'

Matthew Doran is a political reporter in the ABC's Parliament House bureau in Canberra

Courageous Women

Philippa McDonald

KAREN HODGES WAS JUST A KID WHEN A BUSHFIRE TORE towards her home in the central west of New South Wales. It was Christmas Day, and her whole family sprang to action. 'I must have been 11 or 12,' she recalls. 'All the men were out on the trucks and we – my mum, aunts and I – were handling the two-way radio. We lost contact with my uncles for several hours and we didn't know if they were alive or not as the fire had run over them.' Her uncles survived. 'I wanted to be on the truck,' Karen says, 'but it wasn't the done thing at the time.'

Four decades on, Karen is not only on the two-way radio, she's in the RFS control centre as the most experienced incident controller in New South Wales. She has led the fight against up to 20 emergency-level bushfires.

In the 2019–20 fire season, she was at the helm, trying to stop what became known as the Gospers Mountain mega-blaze, one of the largest bushfires in the world to have started from a single ignition point.

The blaze, which was sparked from a lightning strike, grew so massive it eventually covered one million hectares and seven local government areas. It raged for 79 days, and Karen was the incident controller for 60 of those days, often working for 16 hours a day. In her hands were the lives of 3000 firefighters.

'I have to say, my whole time within the RFS, the fire behaviour on this particular time was very erratic,' Karen says. 'Nothing we did stopped it. It was a sleeping giant at the very beginning. We had some rainfall and it went to sleep. But as soon as the weather turned again, it reared its head again. It was a continuous beast. We had what they call the pyrocumulus storms, where the fire was creating its own firestorm and we had that on several occasions on the fire ground. That's something we haven't experienced much in the past at all.'

The hot, dry conditions were relentless. Efforts to slow the blaze even in the middle of the night were for naught. Streams and rivers had run out of water, making aerial firefighting difficult in remote areas. Nothing could hold it back, not even fire trails that had held during previous bushfires in the area.

And it wasn't just the fire itself that the RFS and locals had to deal with. 'There was the tiredness,' Karen says, 'there was fatigue, but there was also hope at times that we would be able to contain the fire. And then when we couldn't, the devastation, disappointment. There were so many people that were trying

RFS superintendent Karen Hodges. (Mridula Amin/ABC)

RFS volunteer Stacey Kent. (Mridula Amin/ABC)

their very best, all the volunteers, the community, the incident management team in here.'

They tried to save every house, but it wasn't always possible and around 100 homes were razed. 'The ones we lost, we were devastated. We look back on it and, talking to the volunteers out there on the day, we're all still dealing with what happened to all the people out there.'

Karen knows the region intimately, having joined the RFS headquarters as an administration officer back in 1988. Within a year she was training to be a firefighter and helping to recruit for the local fire brigade.

But she quickly realised that change had to happen within the RFS. 'It was at the field day,' she recalls, 'where the brigades were competing against each other, running scenarios with the equipment and trucks. The ladies got chocolates and the men got trophies for their participation. I wasn't impressed and I changed that.'

There were no uniforms for women so they designed their own.

By 1990 Karen was the first woman to ever be appointed to the position of deputy fire control officer. She found herself in conflict with some of her fellow firefighters.

'I had to convince the men I would be OK on the fire ground, that I wouldn't kill someone. There was a bunch of old timers in one brigade and they wouldn't let me present them with their medals because they wouldn't take them from a girl.'

Thankfully, she says, her boss was a very good mentor. Karen rose through the ranks and within a decade, at the urging of 21 brigade captains, she successfully applied for the role of fire control officer.

The job is not always easy, particularly when fighting a mega-blaze, but Karen finds inspiration in the people she works with. 'It's the volunteers that keep me going,' she says. 'They come and do it for free and I think, *wow*. And on those bad, dark days we looked out for each other.'

One of those volunteer firefighters is 26-year-old Stacey Kent, who was deployed to fight the Gospers Mountain mega-blaze.

Stacey was motivated to join the RFS because she had friends affected by the 2009 Black Saturday bushfires in Victoria. 'I joined on my sixteenth birthday,' Stacey says, 'and I've loved it ever since.'

She did 120 shifts during the bushfire season, 40 of them virtually in her own back yard, fighting the Gospers Mountain fire. Her footage of driving through what appears to be a firestorm is extraordinarily frightening. 'I was a frontline firefighter. We would be doing anything from putting out spot fires to property protection.'

But nothing could prepare her for what she and her crew from the Round Corner brigade would experience on one horrific day when the firestorm erupted around them.

'Just walls of flame, and as far as you could see, from the treetops up to the sky, and [it] was just orange no matter where you looked. And dark from all the smoke … it was just a wall of flame coming at you.'

Stacey's day job is as a neo-natal intensive care nurse, which means when she's not fighting fires, she's saving babies. She's a kind of angel, a superhero.

'It's pretty full on. I was doing night shifts at the hospital and then doing day shifts on the fire ground,' she says. 'Or doing day shifts at the hospital, night shifts on the fire ground and day shifts at the hospital. So I had two full-time shift-work jobs, essentially.'

Under Karen Hodge's command, Stacey and her fellow RFS firefighters waged an almighty battle to prevent the mega-blaze taking a run towards Sydney's northwestern suburbs. Their goal was keep the fire on the northern side of the Hawkesbury River.

Despite massive flare-ups, they worked day and night putting in backburning operations to try to contain it.

'If we couldn't hold it,' Stacey says, 'it would have jumped the river and come into the Hills District and it would have gone through Maroota, Glenorie – encroached into suburbia really.

'You were just praying and hoping that what you were doing was enough to hold it. If it crossed the river, though, it was going to be catastrophic.'

Evacuation centres across Castle Hill and Baulkham Hills were established in clubs and the area's biggest shopping centre, but in the end the firefighters were successful.

'I'd like to say thank you to a lot of people,' Stacey says. 'We'd show up in these areas and there were people who had lost their homes or potentially could lose homes that were still coming out to support us and give us water and make sure that we were doing OK. The generosity and support that the public had for the firefighters really showed the best of that Australian mateship.'

Karen and Stacey represent the changing face of the fight against bushfires. They were pivotal in the mighty effort to contain one of our biggest fires, which was within a day of reaching Sydney's urban fringe. With future bushfires forecast to be even more frequent and catastrophic, it's heartening to know we have such courageous women leading the battle and standing on the front line protecting us.

During 2019 and 2020, Philippa McDonald covered the bushfires and bushfire recovery for the ABC

The Clean-up

Tom Joyner

MAJOR TOM MACLEAN STOOD AT THE END OF THE ENTRANCE road to the wildlife sanctuary and inhaled deeply. It was barely mid-morning but he'd been up since dawn and could already feel the familiar prickle of his neck beginning to burn.

Across from him, the paddock hummed with activity. Virtually overnight, the area had been transformed into a makeshift base for almost a hundred Australian soldiers in preparation for a long day of clean-up. The mercury read 24 degrees, but – surrounded by blackened tree trunks and the thick scent of ash – it felt warmer.

Since late December, Kangaroo Island had been on fire. Blazes were dampened early on, but a sharp turn in the weather meant a fire in the north burst containment lines in January and tore down the west coast. In less than a month, nearly half the island had been incinerated.

On Sunday, 12 January, all that remained of the Hanson Bay Wildlife Sanctuary – a sprawling conservancy of more than 2000 hectares on the remote southwest of the island – were the burnt-out shells of a visitors' centre, some offices and a cluster of sheds. Water tanks had buckled from the heat of flames; sheets of corrugated roofing lay twisted in a heap. Hectares of bushland further to the south were scorched.

The sanctuary was cofounded 22 years ago by Atlanta-based financier Jim Geddes on what was previously land used for grazing livestock. 'When we came here 22 years ago there were ten kangaroos for every sheep,' Jim tells me that afternoon as we stand under a tree next to the remains of the visitors' centre. 'So we got rid of the sheep.'

Jim, a softly spoken man in his 60s, had returned urgently from the US on Thursday to find his life's work in ruins. Ten days prior, his staff had counted 100 koalas living in the area around the visitors' centre. Today, it was unclear how many had survived.

The last time Jim had seen anything similar was in 2007 when an enormous bushfire burnt through much of Flinders Chase, a wilderness area abutting the sanctuary. By his estimation, this summer's fires had easily covered an area two, perhaps three times larger.

—

Across from where Major Tom Maclean now stood, half a dozen armoured vehicles were parked on the grass, their back doors swung open with uniformed men and women huddled in their shade. A jovial man had set up a truck under some nearby trees and was serving lime cordial and tea.

Tom, a slender and affable man who in a previous life was a reporter for Channel Nine, was in charge of a small team of photographers and videographers sent to document the activities of the army on the island.

He took in the scene before him. Since being posted to Kangaroo Island the week before, he'd seen the char of the landscape and the anguish of locals. As an army public affairs officer, part of his job was to act as a liaison between army personnel and the legion of journalists who had descended on the island since the fires had broken out.

Over the previous months, major European and American television networks and newspapers dispatched reporters to cover the unfolding story of Australian devastation. One German broadcaster had, somewhat remarkably, sent a team of five to Kangaroo Island: a reporter from one of its Asian bureaux, a camera operator and sound recordist, an editor waiting back at the hotel for the day's footage to arrive, as well as a local fixer. NBC News in New York sent a team of three.

At a separate wildlife sanctuary near the centre of the island, a journalist from UK broadcaster ITV found brief viral fame when she was pranked by a straight-faced Australian camera operator and sanctuary staff. 'I'm a bit worried about why I need this level of protection,' she said to the camera warily as she was helped into body armour (in fact a backwards motocross suit) and goggles before a staff member placed a sleepy koala in her arms. It was then that she turned to the camera and delivered her credulous report: 'We've been told this is quite a dangerous bear that's been known to attack people. It's called a drop bear.'

By mid-January, it was clear Australia's Black Summer had become an international symbol of human-induced climate change. Audiences worldwide opened their wallets to donate to volunteer firefighting services as images of injured wildlife and towering flame walls flooded their news feeds.

Tom was staying at the temporary base set up by the army on a football oval in Parndana, a small rural outpost at the island's centre. It was from there that hundreds of soldiers were deployed each day to aid with tasks all over the island. With the worst of the fires now behind them, many locals had turned their attention to recovery.

The army's instructions on the island were to offer assistance wherever it was needed at the request of locals – clearing roads, moving supplies and supporting volunteer firefighters. In the evenings, they'd eat together in the enormous mess tent erected near the basketball courts of the town's only school.

The soldiers' presence was felt almost immediately in Parndana. A usually quiet café on the town's main road adjoining a modest IGA supermarket suddenly found itself overrun when, on Sunday morning, dozens of soldiers poured through the door to order food during their grocery runs. When the growing queue for coffee orders started to overwhelm staff, an army reservist with training as a barista offered his help.

—

It is a horrifying truth that fire itself is only responsible for a fraction of all wildlife deaths. Animals, fearful of the approaching inferno, will try to flee. Some are trapped by flames and roasted alive. Others survive the fire, but what comes next is just as perilous. Their habitat now all but destroyed, they die of starvation or in their weakened state become easy prey.

It was this second wave of animals that Geddes and his team were now faced with rescuing. A handful of koalas remained in the trees surrounding the visitors' centre and were being assessed and treated by vets. A group of soldiers set themselves up in the back of a truck, cradling distressed koalas and feeding them from plastic syringes. Swapping glances, they cooed and grinned at their charges.

Another team of soldiers had been tasked with a far grimmer job: to dig a burial pit for the animals that had died in the first wave.

Coordinating the grim task on behalf of the army was a burly commanding officer by the name of Major Anthony Purdy, who described the situation as 'obviously unpleasant'.

That afternoon, in sweltering heat, rows of soldiers combed bushland around the remains of the visitors' centre. The fire had long been extinguished, but had left behind kilometres of stricken timber that exploded into small clouds of ash underfoot.

The soldiers piled the carcasses of animals that hadn't survived the flames into wheelbarrows, dragging larger remains along the ground by the tail or leg. From a distance, limbs jutted from the wheelbarrows at rigid angles. Fur was singed in some cases and totally evaporated in others. Smaller critters, now almost entirely unrecognisable, were left stacked beside a fence ready to be taken to the pit.

Included in the haul were a number of birds, which gave an indication of the speed and ferocity of the fire front; not even the birds had had time to escape. By Sunday afternoon the remains of some 700 kangaroos, wallabies, koalas and birds were interred there.

Kangaroo Island will hopefully survive these terrible fires and the subsequent threats to livelihoods that Covid-19 has brought. Our defence force, taking on some of the most harrowing jobs in the bushfire clean-up, have made a huge contribution to that recovery.

Tom Joyner is a journalist for 7.30

Dispatched Far and Wide

Jennifer McCutcheon

I LIVE IN DUBBO, WHERE THE ONGOING DROUGHT MEANT that in 2019 there wasn't much to burn. Over the summer, I saw regional communities that were struggling through the worst drought in living memory still managing to rally for other communities impacted by the bushfire crisis. Whether it was by organising a clothing drive, hosting a fundraiser or volunteering their time, these people put their own hardships aside to help others. Countless rural fire volunteers walked away from their farms, jobs and families over Christmas to go and help. Crews from Dubbo, Trangie, Narromine, Wilcannia, Gilgandra and Coonamble were dispatched every week to help fight fires in places like Tenterfield, Jenolan Caves and the New South Wales south coast.

Winemaker James Manners was one such RFS volunteer who found himself fighting fires far from his home in Mudgee.

'I don't see a distinction. I joined to help out – whether it's my community or somewhere else, you join to help,' he told me. 'It's such a hard thing to explain to your family, it's almost impossible. I have two young boys – 14 and 11. They think it's pretty cool, but my wife is a bit different, especially if I go away with a strike team. At the end of the day you're just helping a community and, deep down, they understand.'

But James admitted it was difficult leaving his family after learning about the deaths of Geoffrey Keaton, 32, and Andrew O'Dwyer, 36, both also fathers of young children. They were killed in December when their truck rolled after being hit by a tree in Sydney's southwest. 'That was really tough,' James said. 'I've also been in a vehicle that was hit by a tree; we had a close call in Tenterfield, we were very lucky to be able to walk away from that one.' He said firefighting can bring joy when you successfully save a house or extinguish a fire, but it also has plenty of lows. 'It's an emotional rollercoaster. You have these great wins, but then you have these enormous losses,' he said.

After giving up his summer to help fight fires, James found himself with time on his hands. Ordinarily he'd have spent late January harvesting his grapes, but his entire crop was destroyed by smoke taint. Around 40,000 tonnes of grapes were lost across Australia during the summer's bushfires. Mudgee was hit hard by smoke coming from the Gospers Mountain fire and, unfortunately, smoke contains many compounds that affect the quality of the grapes and can taint the wine.

James Manners on the side of Mount Vincent near Ilford, NSW.
(Photo supplied by James Manners)

'It really hit hard. It was a double whammy, but it was always in the back of my mind. Every day after fighting fires, you'd drive home and see Mudgee shrouded in smoke and this is how it played out, the smoke taint has forced us not to harvest.'

His home was safe, his family too, there hadn't been a fire in sight. Who would have thought smoke would ruin his livelihood after he'd given so much time for others? But James was looking on the bright side. 'I'm now hopefully getting some brownie points back by being a good house-husband and looking after my wife and the kids, cooking dinner and so on.'

—

RFS Group Captain Mark Hoskinson left his farm near West Wyalong in November to help fight fires. I met him in Tamworth – over six hours' drive from his home – where he'd been deployed to fight a grass fire near Moonbi. 'It's the least we can do,' he told me. 'We've had fires in our back yard and people have come to help us out, so we have to repay the favour.' It also gave him some much-needed purpose. The drought had rolled into another year and with nothing to harvest, helping fight fires took Mark's mind off the dry, barren land on the farm. 'It's pretty miserable out at home. Where we are out near West Wyalong, we've had three crop failures and it's pretty bad, so it's good to get away and take your mind off things.'

—

Neal Reed is a school principal in Gilgandra. He's also the deputy captain of the local fire station, and just days before Christmas he was deployed to the fire front at Jenolan Caves, over four hours away. This meant leaving his wife, Jess, to look after their young kids on her own. 'It was a short discussion and all credit to Jess for saying yes,' he said. 'For me there was a sense of purpose but it's always those support people in life who I think bear the real brunt of the time away.' He was able to surprise his family briefly on Christmas Day, but the overall holiday period was not easy. 'It was quite a disrupted Christmas,' he said, his voice beginning to crack. 'It didn't feel like Christmas, we didn't have that downtime. We just rolled into the next thing and it definitely took a toll.'

He was deployed to Jenolan Caves, which sits at the bottom of a spectacularly winding road in the Greater Blue Mountains Heritage Area. This labyrinthine limestone cave structure is significant to the Gundungurra and Wiradjuri peoples, and in 1866 it was set aside for conservation preservation.

Neal said that while he was on deployment there it was very isolating at times. 'Jenolan Caves was interesting because there was no way out or in, once we were in – and I didn't tell Jess that until I returned home. It was like we were in a bubble, because everything was happening around us, the communication lines were down and you were just in this no man's land. The world carried on, but we were just in this space, trying to stay safe.'

Neal spent most of the holidays fighting to save the historic Jenolan Caves site. Ultimately his team was successful. In times of devastation, we so often reflect on the loss, but Neal chooses to focus on the positives. 'That was a win,' he said of saving Jenolan Caves, 'and in the moment you don't think about the gravity of that, but it's on reflection that you do – and you think you're part of something quite special. And that's the legacy of that Christmas–New Year period: there was a lot of loss but so many saves.'

Jennifer McCutcheon is a news reporter based in Dubbo

Emergency Services

Daniel Doody

It was a summer we won't forget. The southeast of New South Wales had been hit by bushfires in the worst possible way. Think of it as several communities all gathered in one circle – and outside that circle was a ring of fire with no end in sight. Many homes were destroyed and people lost their lives, animals were displaced and a sense of terror etched itself into our minds.

I live on the south coast and had been a volunteer with the State Emergency Services (SES) for more than two years. When I had days off from reporting on the fires with the ABC, I felt I couldn't sit around at home and do nothing, so I would put on my orange SES overalls and offer support where I could. My wife, Joanne, was pregnant with our first child, and during the worst period of the fires, she stayed with my parents in Sydney.

Daniel Doody. (ABC Image)

The SES has units located in Bermagui, Bega and Eden – and they all swung into action to support the RFS. We were tasked with carrying out logistics including radio communications, and helping out at evacuation centres across the Bega Valley. Many volunteers were instrumental in helping our community, even when their own homes were destroyed by the fires. For many emergency service workers, it was such an emotional rollercoaster ride, but we banded together to be there for the community that needed us the most.

One particular task the SES, police and the Volunteer Rescue Association (VRA) focused on was door-knocking across the Bega Valley. The RFS had provided volunteers like me with a special message for the members of the community. We had to tell them that if they were going to stay and defend their property, they had to be mentally and physically capable – and if they weren't, we had to make them aware of several evacuation centres in the region.

For us SES members it was mentally and physically challenging – a feat recognised by the SES commander for the Sapphire Coast, Michelle De Friskbom, when she said later: 'performing this task and seeing people at their home … not knowing if they had made the right decision was emotionally difficult to bear'.

From multiple evacuations to the fear of fires coming through our towns and villages, it was certainly overwhelming. But throughout it all, we persevered, and our determination to support our friends at the RFS and help our community members was at the forefront for us.

I am proud of my fellow ABC South East team for their professionalism and for providing vital information to our communities, and also of the SES for their commitment in serving the community under difficult circumstances. Well done and thank you to the RFS, emergency services, local councils and volunteer organisations for keeping us safe.

Daniel Doody is a reporter for ABC South East NSW

COMMUNITY & RESILIENCE

As I ran out of the surf club, it dawned on me that the sun should be up. It was after 7 am. But, instead, the sky above me was pitch-black, with a red glow coming from the west.

The Bermagui Beach Hotel was also accepting a steady stream of evacuees and I found Yannis at the pub, putting out cups of tea and coffee and offering people somewhere comfortable to sit. I breathed a deep sigh of relief as Yannis and I locked eyes, comforted by the fact we were no longer separated. I knew then I would not be letting him out of my sight again.

Our business partners, Luke and Lou, were also there with their extended family, who had just fled from the family farm at Quaama. They were red-eyed and racked with nerves after fighting the fire from all directions throughout the night – thankfully saving their house.

People were clutching their children and dogs, listening to the ABC and refreshing the Fires Near Me app in total disbelief about what was happening. It was a waiting game. 'The fire is 20 minutes from Bermagui,' someone remarked as they walked past me.

By 9 am the sun had started to rise and, in doing so, had turned the sky an ominous orange. Directly above, a pyrocumulus cloud started forming – ash and debris were falling thick and fast. The ash and smoke clung to the back of my throat, feeling lumpy, like an infection. Bits of ash were flying into my eyes and I could barely see where I was going as tears rolled down my cheeks.

At around 10 am, the wind suddenly changed. It was no longer a hot, howling westerly, but a cooler, southerly wind, the kind that always hits the coast after swelteringly hot days.

The wind stopped the fire dead in its tracks – saving Bermagui for the first of what would be many more times to come.

In the lead-up to the next catastrophic fire danger day, authorities advised tourists and residents to leave the town en masse. The fire threat to the town was deemed so severe that most of the services were evacuated. I watched in horror – but also understanding – as most of the SES, surf lifesavers and even the police left. The only authority left in the town was the RFS, which was flogging its guts out to protect the 300 to 400 people who had chosen, or were forced by road closures, to stay.

Yannis and I were asked by the Bermagui RFS to stay and help defend key assets in the town. We had a quick induction on how to use a hose and were lent some uniforms that were well past their use-by dates. We spent the next 24 hours preparing hoses, sprinklers and buckets of water around the pub, steadying ourselves should the fire bear down on us. I felt sick with nervousness and anxiety.

Hot, burnt leaves fell on us that first Saturday after New Year's Eve – but the fire never came. Once again, the southerly wind change came at just the right time and Bermagui was spared.

Claire Wheaton

The Battle for Batlow

Nick Hose

WHAT I KNEW ABOUT BATLOW I COULD'VE SCRIBBLED ON AN A5 notepad. In fact, in one word: 'apples'.

I had barely dusted off my Akubra after four years as a reporter in the Northern Territory when I was sent to report from the fire front. It was my first assignment for *7.30*, the ABC's flagship current affairs program. It was only five days into the new year but it hadn't been a good start.

Batlow, the picture-perfect postcard town in southern New South Wales, famous for its orchards, pine plantations and friendly locals – and apples – had not been spared the devastation that tore through places such as Cobargo and Conjola on New Year's Eve.

Travelling with me were cameraman Shaun Kingma and sound recorder Spiros Mavrangelos. Shaun was a former politics cammo at Parliament House and a part-time DJ. He could be

Camera operator Shaun Kingma and journalist Nick Hose getting ready to report from Batlow, NSW.
(Spiros Mavrangelos/ABC)

counted on for always finding the closest McDonald's and was a reliable source of solid disco bangers in the car. Spiros was a generation older than both Shaun and myself. Calm under pressure, he was a reassuring presence when things got tense, which they did, not far out of Tumut.

'Let's put our fire gear on, guys,' Spiros said in a whisper.

We pulled over and changed into our orange jackets and pants on the side of the road. Just as we were about to get back into the car, another car pulled over beside us. Inside was a mother with two young boys strapped into car seats.

'These men are firefighters,' she explained to her sons, who were both holding identical tyrannosaurus rex figurines.

It wouldn't be the first time that summer we were mistaken for RFS volunteers, despite having 'Media' emblazoned on the backs of our jackets, and usually holding a camera or mic.

Shaun and I politely explained we worked for the ABC and were heading into Batlow. The mother told us she had spent the night alone with her young boys and was now heading to her brother's house to ride out the next few days. I could tell she was frightened. But she was trying her best to hide her fear from her children.

'The worst is over now, isn't it?' she asked us.

—

Local RFS crews had warned us that the road into Batlow was bad, but nothing could have prepared us for the devastation of a firestorm. Spiros had reported from Rwanda and witnessed unspeakable horrors, but the sight of burnt animals melted into the road still hit a nerve.

A herd of cows from a farm that ran alongside the road had ripped through a barbed-wire fence as they tried to escape the flames in their paddock. They hadn't stood a chance. Their bodies were now bloated with gases that made us retch.

Men from the farm were scraping them off the asphalt with a bobcat. We pulled over and covered our faces with whatever we could find to escape the smell. As we grabbed our gear to start taking pictures one of the men yelled out, 'Fuck off, you wankers.'

It was a polarising moment. We were there to tell the story of this town. But I also needed the town to want us to be there.

As we climbed back into the car and drove through the remaining pine forest on the outskirts of Batlow, it reminded me of the Swamp of Sadness from the 1984 film *The NeverEnding Story*. Everything was dead.

And we didn't have Artax the horse to help us.

—

Jay Twemlow was expecting us. His face was covered in charcoal and his eyes were red. He looked like he'd visited hell. It occurred to me later that no one we'd met that day had slept the night before. Still, Jay greeted us with a friendly handshake, welcoming us like he was the mayor. 'Sorry about the road,' he said.

We met up across the road from a burnt-out petrol station that had exploded in the firestorm. The force of the explosion had sent metal high into the sky.

'He's a good bloke, that servo bloke,' Jay said, and told us how the night before, as the fire approached, the petrol station attendant had risked his life to open up so locals could fill their generators. That was all some people were now relying on.

Jay had done all he could to try and save the town. He'd teamed up with some other locals and worked out a strategy: start at opposite ends of a street and work towards the middle. They saved seven homes that night.

Jay told us some locals had sheltered on the oval, before that came under threat when the wind changed direction. For many, the last place of refuge was the 99-year-old Batlow Hotel. But it was no celebration. One person died that night and more than 20 homes were lost.

'You just follow the flames and wherever you see black skies you drive into it,' Jay said. 'It's basically pure hell.'

As Jay was driving through Batlow putting out spot fires, he noticed an elderly woman and her brother sitting in their back yard. Their plan was to hide out in the cellar. It was a decision that might have cost them their lives. As the fire roared towards their home, Jay urged them to evacuate instead.

We went back with Jay to find the woman he'd saved. She thanked him for his help and asked him if he could reattach the gas so she could have a cup of coffee. Of course, Jay did.

—

Over the next few days, as emergency crews worked to clear roads and make the town safe, travel into Batlow was getting harder. Our ability to tell the story of the town depended largely on the RFS volunteers waving us through the checkpoints on our way in from nearby Tumut, where we were staying. Some saw the ABC logo and wished us well; others would pore over the paperwork or call over more senior members for advice. These volunteers had a job to do, and it was our job to support them, but I felt anxious approaching a roadblock and I was always relieved to get through.

Getting into the town meant that I was seeing which houses had survived and which had been burnt before their evacuated owners were allowed to go in themselves.

Max Gordon Hall was the local paramedic. His home was the very last place at the end of a quiet street that backed onto a state forest. He described it as 'a little slice of paradise'. Max, a young man, had moved to Batlow for work and instantly fallen in love with the town. The house was the first he'd ever

The fire in Batlow destroyed more than 20 homes. (Nick Hose)

Jay Twemlow at the Batlow petrol station. (Nick Hose)

bought. He'd worked hard on improving it. A new sunroom, for starters. After spending many weekends wrestling the wild berry bushes that crept up from the forest and into his yard, he'd eventually bought himself a ride-on mower.

Max was in Japan when Australia's Black Summer bushfire crisis hit the New South Wales south coast. Each night he watched on the Fires Near Me app as small local blazes crept closer and closer to his house. I'm not sure he really believed those small fires would reach other small fires and eventually form a mega-blaze the likes of which no one had seen before. That seemed unimaginable in November 2019, but by January 2020 it felt like the whole country was on fire.

From the safety of Japan, Max watched the relentless coverage of fires that were tearing through communities just like his. When Batlow came under threat, he knew it was time to come home. Max and I spoke for the first time on the phone, and when he described the location of his house, I was almost certain it would have been burnt to the ground. But I didn't let on.

Shaun, Spiros and I arranged to meet Max in Tumut, but first we had a short discussion about how much we would tell him. Once Max knew his house was probably gone, it was likely he'd pull out of the story. We decided it was only ethical to brief him fully.

When you're a reporter, it's part of your job to form instant connections with total strangers. Leigh Sales once said you have to fall in love with your subjects, and I guess in a way with

Max I did. He was a good person. He cared about his town, and his role as a paramedic in keeping people safe, and he wore that care on his sleeve like a badge of honour.

After we told him about his house, there was a long pause. We leant against our car and gave him some time. 'I just want to know if my ride-on mower is OK,' he said finally. It was a Christmas present to himself. Knowing he wouldn't be allowed into Batlow, we hustled him into yellow fireproof gear and put him in the back of our ABC car.

We had driven in and out of Batlow numerous times by now and were becoming desensitised to the Swamp of Sadness. But driving through that empty dead forest and experiencing it again through Max's eyes brought the reality home for a second time. Max wasn't used to seeing the apple orchards burnt, the sign welcoming people to Batlow ripped apart by fire, or the petrol station broken into tiny pieces of twisted metal. He was in shock.

As we rounded the corner to his street, he said, 'I won't know until I get to that dirt patch if my home is still standing.'

In a few moments, I thought to myself, your life will never be the same again. Silence descended over the car as Max saw his home black and flattened. 'Holy mackerel,' was all he could manage.

We sat there quietly until finally he took control of the moment and, releasing his seat belt, said, 'Should we go take a look?'

Max Gordon Hall at the remains of his Batlow home. (Nick Hose)

As a paramedic, Max witnesses and deals with trauma for a living, but now he was the one experiencing the trauma. As he surveyed the damage, he said things like, 'All that work for nothing,' and 'This is where the bedroom was.' But he was also good-humoured at times, laughing at the bitter irony of a woodpile surviving while his house had not.

It wasn't until he got to his shed and saw his ride-on mower that he lost it. The mower had been completely destroyed. All the weekends Max had spent fixing roofs, painting, building, and weeding wild berries that scratched him and made him bleed … It was all gone, and all he had to show for it was a burnt-out mower.

My natural instinct was to reach over and comfort him, but my job was to document what was happening to the people of Batlow. And grief and loss were part of that story.

As we began to wrap up for the day, state authorities arrived. They told Max that the local RFS had made the very difficult decision to sacrifice his home to save the street. Max said he understood. He was just happy the street had been saved.

—

On our last night in Tumut, Shaun, Spiros and I made our way to the local pub. We ordered steaks and beers and sat in the main dining hall. As luck so often has it in small towns, Max and his girlfriend sat at a table near us.

A light rain fell over Tumut that night, not enough to put out the fires but enough to bring hope. One by one, more and more locals crashed into the dining hall, wet from the rain. Quickly the pub filled with farmers, RFS volunteers and locals enjoying a pint. It felt like the whole community was there.

Tumut and Batlow are ABC towns and I was pleased to see a giant screen in the dining hall with the ABC News channel playing. We tucked into our steaks and I asked the waitress if we could turn up the volume to watch *7.30*.

As she got the remote, I suddenly began to feel sick. It occurred to me that the story that Shaun, Spiros and I had shot, edited and filed was the story of the very people in this room. It was about their town, their experience, their sadness, their loss, their hope. Images from only this morning were now beaming into people's living rooms across Australia, and into this pub.

The room fell silent – no easy feat in a roaring country pub. I surveyed the room, catching Max's eye. The ego of being the reporter on the TV left me, and I began to worry about how Max must be feeling, surrounded by his peers in the pub as he told his story of loss on national television, even weeping over a ride-on mower.

As the piece finished, the room erupted in applause. People held up their beers in salute to Max. I had never felt so emotional watching a story of mine before, but, in truth, it wasn't my story. It was the story of Batlow. Not a story of apples and orchards and pine plantations, but a story of kindness and care and unfathomable resilience.

A few weeks later, I found out that a farmer in a nearby town had donated her ride-on mower to Max. It didn't surprise me, for this was the true never-ending story, not with a swamp of sadness, but an ocean of compassion.

Nick Hose is a journalist at 7.30

Building Community in a Scorched Summer

Baz Ruddick

I'M 14 YEARS OLD AND I'M RUNNING FOR THE SCHOOL BUS. There's a mist coming off Narira Creek. Thin and wispy. The air is cold in my lungs. I've just said goodbye to my mum with a kiss on the cheek. I've stepped over the sleeping dog lying in the doorway to the main bar and made my way out the front door of the pub. I've left behind the smell of stale beer, which will trigger deep nostalgia when I am older. In four years' time I will leave Cobargo and not look back.

—

I've always been a believer that community isn't automatic. Our default can be to avoid associating with people and retreat into the safety and protection of our own families. In the 2019–20 summer I saw fires pull people out of their homes and push them together. It affected everyone differently, but linked all communities in the same way, no matter where they were. I saw a natural disaster pull people down and bring them together at the same level. A pursuit of survival and hope.

Bushfire first came into my life when I was a child. I was too small to remember but repeated oral history has solidified the events in my mind with such unshakeable foundations that I may as well have been on the back of a ute pointing a hose. A three-year-old in a tiny yellow jumpsuit, with an ashen face and the determination of a man trying to save the family house. Three-year-old Baz to the rescue!

In reality, our farming neighbours pulled together with a backburning operation and saved our house from a fast-moving grass fire. Fences had to be cut to move stock after my own clueless father had locked gates and lost keys.

There was always a certain terror in my mother's voice as she recounted those events – a particular emotion that I didn't hear in anyone else's voice for many years. But in late 2019 and early 2020 I heard it again and again, from people I knew and people I was meeting for the first time.

I grew up above the Cobargo Hotel. My step-dad was the publican and my mum was his right-hand everything. She had a reputation among the locals as a proper lady. She didn't drink. She was polite, friendly and served anyone with the sort of warmth that made you feel like you were coming home. If you mucked up, she put you on a 'no spirits list'. She was convinced that rum released the raging devil. If you mucked up too badly, my step-dad would step in. He would ban drinkers willingly and liberally.

The Cobargo I knew in my youth was a divided place. It was deeply rural with strong dairy-farming roots and old families who had made their livelihoods in the valley for more than a century. It was also flamboyantly eccentric and alternative. Hippies, greenies and those looking for an alternative way of living flocked to the beautiful and quiet surrounds of the town.

I was an observer back then. Hanging out the window of the pub watching the world go by. Getting up in the middle of the night to see the odd barney on the highway. My first foray into journalism was recounting those fights to mates at school.

Then in December 2019, I was again an observer of the town of Cobargo. This time from my work desk. I sat in the studio of ABC Southern Queensland in Toowoomba while on the TV above me images of the main street of our idyllic village going up in flames played on repeat. Seeing my hometown burning from across the country was a bizarre experience. But it wasn't the first fire I'd seen that season.

In September 2019, I watched a parched and tinder-dry Stanthorpe in southern Queensland come under direct threat. My colleagues and I at ABC Southern Queensland had already been reporting on the region heavily and the Granite Belt had hit national headlines multiple times that year. It had become the poster child for the severity of one of the longest and most widespread droughts the country had seen. The town that was running out of water completely.

On 6 September, the day that fire hit, we'd sat poised in the newsroom. The forecast was for high winds, high temperatures and low humidity. A day of catastrophic fire danger, officials said. We knew it was coming, but we just didn't know where in our large broadcast area it would spark.

Late in the afternoon it started. Like the snap of a whip, coming through the crackling emergency radio scanner, you could hear the town jump to action. With emergency broadcasting underway, I left the studio in Toowoomba, hoping the fire would die down overnight, and went home to prepare for an early morning trip to Stanthorpe.

Roads were closed that morning and reports of damage varied. Many had lost sheds. Some had lost homes. Anyone who has seen the aftermath of a fire will attest to the random nature of the destruction. Why was that home spared and not that one? Why did that heap of wood survive but that tin shed go up in flames?

At a Salvation Army shop in Stanthorpe I met Brad and Coral Krahe, who'd been asleep when the fire came dangerously close to their house. Alerted by an emergency text message, a neighbour pounded on the door and woke them up. The couple bundled up their pets and spent the night in their car as their home burnt. Then they went to their local Salvos to pick out clothes to replace the only ones they had – those on their back. Brad was happy with his new aesthetic. He blushed and then beamed as I told him he looked like Carlos Santana, the famous guitarist. They could be anyone they wanted now, I said. A whole new look.

As I asked them what had happened the previous night, Brad and Coral sat in a sort of serene state of shock. After the interview we took a photo. 'Okay, can you please drop your smiles?' I asked. Again I asked the same thing. And again.

They looked tired, but not like they had been dragged to hell and back. There was a certain lightness to the situation you wouldn't expect and couldn't predict. Did the fire lift the heaviness of reality from their backs? They were out of danger. They were alive. Maybe it was an example of living completely in the present.

My ABC colleagues and I spoke to people who had lost everything and we spoke to people who had saved it all, the result of a mixture of sheer hard work, help from elsewhere – and luck. But the irony was that even for families who had saved their homes and farms, the dry continued to take it away, slowly and sadistically. In mid-January, trucks began ferrying water from Warwick's Leslie Dam to Stanthorpe's Storm King Dam.

Living in the country can be a gamble. Nature and weather can and do take it all. The first bit of rain I saw, months later, came in the form of millions and millions of broad-bean-sized hail stones, dumped in such large volumes they shredded protective nets that hung over orchards or massed into two-cubic-metre sagging heaps that pulled the nets away and exposed the fruit below to the icy bullets.

As the New Year rolled around, natural disasters continued. And then on the morning of New Year's Eve 2019 the main street of Cobargo was hit by a holocaust.

Within two days I was on a plane bound for my hard-hit home. I felt like a reinforcement, coming in to help the ABC's South East NSW crew in Bega. It felt like a service. If the south coast was going to go through a natural disaster I wanted to be there. I wanted to tell those stories.

Flying into the south coast was heartbreaking. Large strips of bush blackened, spot fires smoking and ant-sized people seeking refuge on strips of sand at the ocean's edge. As we flew, I did a tally on my fingers. Nine. At that stage, at least nine people I knew had lost homes and livelihoods. Mostly people I had gone to school with. They had seen their childhood homes reduced to ash. At the time, this seemed remarkable, but after the event, it was just another typical south coast experience from that summer.

As a journalist you look for the hardest angle, the case study that will illustrate the situation at its most extreme. Finding this person can often be challenging, but this time it wasn't. Destruction and loss were nearly the rule rather than the exception.

I didn't have to look far. Familiar faces from my hometown had seen it all. I caught up with an old mate from school, Jack Wotton, who told me his story. His parents, Swampy Tom and Sharyn, had spent 16 years building their property from scratch using salvaged materials. It was in Wandella, west of Cobargo. On 30 December, with fire approaching, the family packed what they could and fled their property for the safety of town. In the early hours of New Year's Eve they fled again under a cloud of smoke and anxiety, this time from the town of Cobargo itself.

On New Year's Day, after the fire had passed through, Jack took his postie bike and snuck away from where the family had sought shelter in nearby Narooma to see how their house had fared. He was the first of the family to see what was left. Under a sepia-toned sky, Jack saw the lifetime project of his parents reduced to a pile of buckled tin and ash. The micro-rainforest around the house was scorched and cooked. The intense heat of the flames had zapped anything green, instantly sucking the moisture away from it, as if the environment had become a kiln.

'When I got back, Dad came out,' Jack told me. 'He had worked out where I had gone when I disappeared. He asked how everything looked and I just said to him, "Hey, we really should have eaten those steaks."' This became a recurring joke between Jack and his dad. They'd lost the house, sure, but they'd also left behind some T-bone steaks in the fridge.

Cobargo's main street, destroyed by the fire that swept through on 31 December 2019. (above: Greg Nelson/ABC; below: Matt Roberts/ABC)

'My girlfriend always says this thing: memories are attached to a place and history is attached to events,' Jack said. 'All those memories that are harboured there are gone and now it is up to us and the people that were there to share those memories.'

The first person he spoke to after seeing the house was his neighbour, who had stayed with his family and defended his home to the very bitter end. The house was saved but there was no joyous relief. 'He said it was his biggest regret putting his family through that trauma,' Jack told me. 'They saved the house but it was proper hell and they were totally surrounded by it.'

When I lived in Cobargo as a kid I'd heard stories about the 1956 fire. Old blokes said it had started in Brogo and travelled more than 50 kilometres through Cobargo then Tilba until eventually hitting the ocean further north. Some say spot fires from the main front even started fires on Montague Island more than six kilometres offshore. It's hard to confirm if this happened, but after seeing the rapid pace of destruction by the fires on the far south coast in 2019–20, I could believe it.

It took nine days before the town of Cobargo looked like an inhabited town. The pub I knew from my youth stood steadfast and strong at the southern end of the bridge. It was a stoic survivor and had become a refuge for many and a place of normality for the traumatised community.

Pictures of locals calling the prime minister every name under the sun had made their way around the globe. But most of the locals didn't know about the extent of the media coverage because most didn't have power. The firefighter who had lost his own home and had famously refused the prime minister's handshake didn't realise he was a celebrity. He was in such a state of shock he hadn't even noticed the cameras.

By 9 January the media storm had taken a breather. My colleague Daniel Doody and I walked the streets of Cobargo. The sky was blue. We could still smell the fire, and logs still smouldered on the outskirts of town, but for the first time since we'd arrived things were lively. There was a hum and a vibration in the air. People were smiling, despite the fact that a melted train carriage stood where a quirky cafe had been and safety fencing blocked off the ruins of several 150-year-old buildings. Locals were cuddling in the street, sitting out the front of shops and participating in the age-old tradition of the bush telegraph. You could say g'day to anyone.

At that point I didn't feel like I was reporting on a disaster. I felt like I was reporting on resilience and survival. It wasn't what had happened, but what was happening now.

Daniel and I headed to the co-operative hardware and agriculture supply store to hear how farmers were getting back to it. The green pasture behind the shop was covered in a fine powdery ash. Staff members told us that fire crews had fought tooth and nail to save the buildings. It was a town asset and that's where the rebuild would begin. Business was bustling. Cars lined up to refuel and pick up feed. Metal fence palings were sold out and so were 1000-litre water cubes. The computer system wasn't up and running so accounts were being run on tick with a pen and paper.

Next we walked over to the bookshop. Despite losing her home, owner Louise Brown had opened for business. A sign in the window read: 'Post-apocalyptic fiction now moved to current affairs'.

A large proportion of properties destroyed in the surroundings of the village were off-grid and possibly not insured. But there was no time to dwell on this. It was much better to have a laugh and carry on.

An evacuation centre had been set up at the showground and was being run at a grassroots level to make sure everyone would be looked after. Even for those who had a place to go back to, the centre had become a congregation point and a new hub for the recovering community. Displaced people set up caravans and a new community was being born.

In the weeks following the fire, my school mate Jack went to the centre many times. 'It is going to be a long march home for everyone,' he told me. 'But a great thing is that people have worked together more now than they have ever before in the past. All kinds of people are helping each other out and a lot of people are benefitting. There are beautiful things going on in Cobargo. You have a community working together and it has to do with our state of mind. Living and breathing together when push comes to shove. It is like breathing and beating humanity.'

This period following the fire was the most amount of time I had spent in Cobargo in thirteen years. When I moved away aged 18, the town hadn't felt special at all, but in this wounded little village I was now seeing a place and a community I wanted to be part of. A place that made me smile. It was always known that Cobargo residents looked after their own, but this was now a more united, tolerant and closer town on all levels, far from its politically and socially divided former self.

What I saw and heard in those days following the devastation was an image of a community better than the one I had left. Or maybe I just hadn't seen it tested.

Baz Ruddick is a reporter at ABC Brisbane, based in Ipswich

FACING THE FUTURE

Halfway through the second week of January, I returned to work at the ABC to help my colleagues cover the ongoing crisis. Most days I was out in the field meeting people who had lost everything and helping them to share their stories. At the end of each day, I would cry while driving the 40 minutes home to Bermagui, watching all the way for active fire along the road.

A fire was still burning on the mountain just a couple of kilometres inland from our house. At night, we could see it from the back of our property – and we would try to measure how much closer it had moved that day.

It felt like death by a thousand cuts and, after evacuating three more times over the next month, we were begging for it to burn us and be done with it. The psychological game just had to end, even if it meant we lost everything, as strange as that is. We couldn't bear the anxiety of waiting any more.

But in the end, it didn't burn us. More than a month after fire first entered our world, it finally left us.

Torrential rain fell and fell and fell – pouring hundreds of millimetres of water onto our blackened, scorched earth. It brought with it new challenges, polluting our estuaries with bushfire run-off and causing the region's dam to fill with debris.

But, overall, people collectively exhaled an enormous life-changing sigh of relief. Suddenly dams that had been empty for 18 months were full. Grass seemed to be growing right in front of our eyes, somewhat hiding the very deep scars that we were all now carrying.

Life as we knew it had changed – and I know that I, for one, will never be the same.

Claire Wheaton

A Place Like Home

Hamish Macdonald with
Karen Michelmore

MARGARET BRUS HAD SPENT MANY AN AFTERNOON ON THE deck of her house, overlooking the water at Batemans Bay on the New South Wales south coast. The patch of small rocky mounds sitting slightly out to sea is a familiar, and reassuring, sight. The locals call it the Toll Gate.

'It is a nature reserve,' Margaret told me. 'If you look at one angle they are split, but if you look at them in another angle they look like they are one. It was just a nice way to spend the afternoon. You'd get the easterly breeze, it was a nice spot.'

The ocean had long been a source of comfort to Margaret, a 64-year-old library technician who moved to Australia with her family from The Netherlands more than 50 years ago. She remembered vividly the first time she saw the Pacific Ocean, after flying into Sydney early one summer morning, along with her six brothers and sisters and her parents. 'It was just the most beautiful thing we had ever seen. It was just like, "Wow. Look at this place. We are in paradise now."'

That first weekend they spent on the beach, jubilant, but they also got their first lesson in Australia's unforgiving sun. 'When we came home we were so sunburnt, we had blisters – nobody told us about sunscreen,' she told me with a smile.

Margaret moved south from her home in Wollongong to the peaceful coastal town of Batemans Bay following the death of her 24-year-old son, Brendon, in 2009. 'He had Duchenne muscular dystrophy and so he was always going to pass away at an early age. I was his main carer and it was just one of those things that happens in life, and he passed away. And I thought it was also a good opportunity for me to, more or less, change environments, you know? Get away from the sadness and start a new life.'

That new life revealed itself after she met Jeff Brooks, a charter-boat operator from Batemans Bay, on an online dating site. And so she made Batemans Bay home. 'It was very quiet, very quiet and I didn't mind it at all,' she said. 'Living in Wollongong it could be quite busy, and I just liked the slower pace.'

She picked up a job at the local library and she and Jeff settled in for what they thought would be a quieter chapter in their lives. But it didn't turn out that way.

I met Margaret on the first few days of January 2020, near the Batemans Bay RSL Club, while I was preparing to go on television and update viewers on the unfolding situation.

'Our home was pretty much gone in the fire,' were her first dazed words to me on air.

—

I grew up in Jindabyne in the Snowy Mountains, and we'd usually go to the south coast of New South Wales for family holidays when I was little. For me, it's home. I've spent most of my adult life and career working overseas as a foreign correspondent, and have spent time in some difficult and dangerous places, so it's always been important to me to have the Snowies to go back to.

There's something about the fresh air when I arrive home. There's a bend when you are coming down the Monaro Highway and you are about to hit East Jindabyne, and you see the whole of Lake Jindabyne and the mountains open up in front of you. I always wind down the windows of the car so, when I see it in that first moment, I can take it all in at the same time. Not just the sight, but the smell and the cold, fresh mountain air. There's something special about it.

I spent Christmas 2019 with my siblings, nieces and nephews at my father's house in Jindabyne. Then a couple of days after Christmas my partner and I drove to Tathra on the New South Wales south coast, to a flat we'd booked for a week's holiday. After a hectic year, we were really looking forward to it. There'd been fires further up the coast but they weren't really on our radar. It didn't seem like they would come anywhere near us and while there was a fair bit of smoke around, we were able to slide into holiday mode – gorging on fresh oysters and prawns, going for swims and playing lazy card games like Asshole on the deck. We didn't have any idea about what was coming. On the night before New Year's Eve, we went for dinner with some friends at the beautiful old Tathra pub. Tathra's a tiny village with huge caravan parks that are always full to the brim over the Christmas period. The town was throbbing. There was a band playing and the pub felt crowded. Signs around the pub advertised the planned New Year's Eve celebrations and we were talking about how we should celebrate. The weather was a bit funny, though. Along with the smoke, the temperature had dropped and there was a fair bit of wind. But there wasn't any sense of panic or imminent danger.

But soon after we arrived back at our holiday flat that night, we received a text from a friend saying there'd been a fire alert for the area, and talk of voluntary evacuations. We jumped online, but we couldn't quite work out whether or not we were in the danger zone, so we set an alarm for 6 am, thinking at least if we were up early we could check the situation then.

When we woke on New Year's Eve we had several missed calls and a few quite panicked messages, and warnings, with screen grabs of RFS updates. On the radio, ABC South East presenter Simon Lauder was repeating the warning, 'If you are anywhere between Bega and Batemans Bay you should consider leaving. If you are going to leave, do it before 8 am.'

A lot of ash was falling from the sky and, although it was early, the sky was glowing red. Kangaroos were grazing on a neighbour's lawn. We followed the advice and left. We could see and smell plumes of smoke as we drove the short 15 minutes west to Bega. It was unsettling finding ourselves suddenly reliant on a range of core services, like the petrol station, local ABC Radio and the Fires Near Me app. You don't realise how dependent you'll become on those things – and how quickly. We felt so grateful for that flow of information and also for people's calmness.

We didn't exactly have a plan. We knew we needed to get to Bega because on the radio the presenters had been saying to head to the emergency evacuation point there. By the time we got to the town all the roads were closed. We couldn't really go anywhere else.

There was a café open, absolutely choc-a-block full of people who had come down from the hills, from properties that had been on fire overnight. People were arriving to see their friends and families and to exchange stories of the night. And there were people clearly feeling pretty strung out and emotional.

We headed to the showground where other people were arriving with their trailers, some with boats. Others had their farm animals. It was a pretty significant movement of people, even though it was before 8 am.

I tweeted a photo of the main street with its threatening skies – and the producers at ABC RN were quickly on the phone wanting to know if they could chat to me on air. Soon after that, I had emails and messages from people in other parts of the ABC wanting to know if I could work.

I did live television crosses throughout the day. As the hours wore on, people in the studio commented on how much worse everything was looking than earlier and that the situation had changed a lot. I was slightly taken by surprise by that and had to take a proper look around for myself. When you are in it, it creeps up slowly.

By 2 pm that day it was somehow both dark as night and bright red at the same time. It was a hellish landscape, but one that was becoming increasingly very real. I asked Bega mayor Kristy McBain if she had everything she needed for the 24 hours ahead and she stopped dead in her tracks and looked at me. She simply said she didn't know. She repeated it two or three times. When the people in charge appear so calm and so dignified in the face of it all and then acknowledge to you that they just don't know what will happen, that almost creates a new reality for you and puts things in perspective.

—

The Princes Highway reopened on 1 January, and my partner and I drove back up to Sydney. We left very early when there was little traffic, but lots of smoke and smouldering trees and bush. It's hard to believe it was New Year's Day, the start of a new year.

As we left the smouldering ruins of towns and lives, it became clear that fires were starting to threaten the area near my father's place at Jindabyne. There were fires approaching from three different directions – including from Kosciuszko National Park, which had been evacuated. Firefighting resources were stretched.

My father is 80 and he's lived in his place longer than I've been alive. The advice from the RFS was that residents in his area could stay and defend, but you needed to be able to defend *vigorously*. My dad's independent, and was very comfortable and happy where he was, but we knew he wasn't up to fighting fires. It was a difficult series of conversations, because he didn't really want to go. The whole process of thinking about leaving and the packing was very stressful for him. We spent quite a while on the phone together, writing out a list of what he might want to pack. All those things that you know you need are often not easy to find in the actual moment. Fortunately, we have family in Canberra who were happy to receive him and, in the end, Dad was happy to go stay with them. We knew he was in good hands.

The experience of evacuating my dad brought a different perspective to the reporting I was doing. I suddenly realised the difficulty of the decisions that everyone was having to make. I realised that even when all the information might be pointing to a straightforward decision to leave, there could be far more complex emotional factors at play.

I returned to the south coast on Friday, 3 January with an ABC crew and got back to work. The following day was forecast to be another impossibly horrible one. I was presenting live rolling coverage for *News 24* from Batemans Bay, crossing to other reporters in the field in different parts of the fire zone, and hosting part of the 7 pm news live each night.

Margaret Brus just turned up one day in between the live television crosses. She was clearly shaken by everything that had happened, but like a lot of people who have gone through something traumatic, she also clearly felt the need to tell us about it. Maybe she was trying to understand it for herself. The whole thing had taken her by surprise – and because my partner and I had also been taken by surprise earlier in the week, I really connected with her story.

It had been a devastating few days for Margaret. The house she and Jeff had lived in all those years, looking out to the ocean, had been reduced to a pile of blackened rubble several days earlier. When they were finally allowed back in, it was a mess. The intensity of the firestorm was clear.

'We were standing there, the first day we went up there, and there's this trail of alloy, like a piece of art in the grass,' she told me. 'It was so intense, the fire, that it melted the alloy wheels.'

The glass in the windowsills also melted, and were now draped over the structure. The items that survived, such as a diver's helmet, felt inexplicably random.

'The dishwasher was even more incredible,' she said. 'I must have had a load in there, but the door must have opened, and there were dishes still in the dishwasher and some of them didn't even look damaged. There was a coffee pot that I bought years and years ago. A white coffee pot. It was standing there not even broken.'

But the thing Margaret was saddest about were the irreplaceable things she'd left behind. After her son, Brendon, died, his mates put together a book with photos, little notes and well wishes. It was sitting in the lower television cabinet with her other photo albums.

'Brendon was very social,' she said. 'He had a lot of able-bodied mates that looked after him and they were fabulous. They were all into this heavy black metal stuff, but they were the nicest group of people you could meet. They put together this book for us when Brendon passed away. At the funeral they handed it to us. It was a nice way for me to remember my son because he was remembered so well by his mates. I just had the caring side of him, that's what I did. But his mates had the fun with him and that was nice to see.

'I forgot to take it with me in the rush of things. You don't think you are going to lose your house. We really were blown away when someone said our house was going, especially when all the other houses around us didn't. You think you are safe.'

Margaret had been subconsciously aware of how dry everything was for months. Batemans Bay was on level-three water restrictions and the grass was crunchy underfoot. Kangaroos had started visiting a small patch of grass kept green by her recycled wastewater.

'The grass around our house was so dry it felt like you were walking on glass. It was so dry and crunchy under your feet. It was no wonder that everything flared up.'

The fires had been in the region since November. They crept closer, and closer, until nearby beach hamlets started being evacuated. The day it came to Batemans Bay, Margaret had been feeling uneasy but was unprepared for any emergency. Her partner, Jeff, had been due to take a group of fishermen out on his charter boat, but decided to cancel. He got up at 4 am to check the tides and weather anyway, and Margaret woke up too.

'I might have got up having a gut instinct, a gut feeling. I got up that morning and I started pacing. I packed the bag. There was so much smoke around. There was a lot of smoke around for days. We got black leaves in the garden. I could smell it.' Her gut had churned. 'I walked down my driveway and I saw a lump of charcoal sitting on my driveway. I was thinking this isn't a leaf, this is a whole chunk. It was like an ember.'

She went to the safety of her sister-in-law's house, while Jeff and his mate Foxy stayed behind to finish preparing the property. Jeff joined Margaret soon after. 'You could see this dark and orange angry cloud just coming from the west down, heading towards where we lived. It didn't look good. I was really worried. It was light and the next minute it was dark. This dark cloud just came across the window. It was like Armageddon, I suppose, and orangeness came behind it.'

In the end it all happened very quickly. Within a few hours they'd received a call that their house was gone. Jeff and Foxy tried to visit the house several times that day and were finally granted access, as long as they reported back so authorities knew they were okay. Jeff told Margaret it was terrible – and that she wouldn't want to see it. But, like Jeff, Margaret needed to see it. She needed to know. 'It's not real until you see it. I walked up there and it is hard to describe how you feel. I think I just burst into tears to start with and then I took some photos for the insurance company.'

The sense of danger didn't leave them for days. Nor the ash, nor the smoke.

'I sat down a lot and cried and drank cups of tea,' Margaret told me, 'because there wasn't much that you could do. It was just really wait and see what happens.'

By the end of our interview, I felt so terribly sad for Margaret that the obvious human thing to do was to ask her if she needed a hug. On reflection, it was probably because I needed a hug as well. My interview with Margaret was a pre-record that was being fed to ABC headquarters, where it would be edited by producers and put to air. I hadn't imagined that they would keep that moment when Margaret and I hugged in there, but they did. Probably as much as any reports I did during those bushfires, that hug seems to have resonated with people.

I think as a nation we all felt pretty helpless, because it was very difficult as a community to see something so terrible happening and feel so unable to prevent it. We probably all needed a collective hug.

—

I checked back in with Margaret three months later and asked after their property.

'It's an absolute mess,' she said. 'There are still sheets of metal everywhere. Jeff had to cut the grass because the grass has grown back beautifully. It's really quite nice. But it's just depressing. Every time you go there, you see it – it's a reminder that this has happened.'

Margaret and Jeff had moved into a nearby rental property, but were considering moving away from the area, possibly to Queensland. A rebuild in Batemans Bay could take years and there was the emotion to consider. 'You just have to move on,' she said. 'That's what you have to do. And staying here at the moment, I'm not so sure that's a good thing. Even a couple of days ago, I drove past the street where the house was – I didn't

Vanessa and Peter Williams, at the site of their house and pottery studio in Mogo, NSW. (Antonette Collins)

Hamish Macdonald, hosting the 7 pm news live from Mogo. (Marton Dobras/ABC)

even go past the house – and I burst into tears. Maybe it's good to get away from it, so it's not the constant reminder there for now.'

The hardest part was the uncertainty. Of not having made a firm decision on what their future would be and where they would live.

'We were very settled,' Margaret said. 'We were sort of in retirement phase, you might say. We had our house, we had no debt. All the things you need in life, our health, and then this happens. And we are back to square one almost. You realise that things can happen. You don't know what is around the corner. You should live in the moment.'

—

We have a tendency in the news business to cover a story in a big way then move on pretty fast and forget that these crises are not single, isolated moments. The impact is long-running and usually the period that comes after it is as difficult as the first traumatic moment.

The long, slow, grinding path to recovery is going to be difficult for these communities. For people like Margaret. And for others like Peter and Vanessa Williams, another couple who lost everything in the fires. They too were going to have to start again. Their property was uninsured, but their home, built lovingly from two old Catholic churches, was irreplaceable anyway.

The circumstances in which I came to meet them were probably not the most flattering. In fact, our ABC television crew must have looked like quite a spectacle when Peter and Vanessa wandered up to us as we prepared to host the 7 pm news live from the tiny hamlet of Mogo, about ten kilometres inland from Batemans Bay.

It was early evening, in early January, just a day or so after their beloved community had been largely razed by fire. Peter and Vanessa had come back to have a look at what was left of their property and agreed to an interview.

Naturally, things didn't go to plan. There was a terrible series of technical failures, which made it all very stressful. With only two or three minutes to go before we were live on air, literally nothing was working. Peter and Vanessa waited patiently during the set-up, perhaps enjoying the strange entertainment.

About 45 seconds before 7 pm, it somehow miraculously came together. I had a satellite phone taped to my back and I was so nervous about the signal failing that I barely moved a millimetre for the entire program.

Finally, with the broadcast over, we could do the interview with Peter and Vanessa. It was only the second time that they had been back to their property to see what had happened and it was impossible not to be carried along with their emotion of seeing what they'd lost.

They told us how they had met in Year 12 at Deakin High School and studied fine arts at university in Melbourne, before moving to Mogo 40 years ago. In early 1980 they heard that St Mary's church on the hill in town was for sale.

'We just couldn't resist the beautiful spot and the beautiful building,' Vanessa told me. 'It was lined with pressed metal completely and it was just gorgeous. We went to the Catholic priest and said, "We'd like to buy this, we heard it was for sale." And he said, "That's not for sale, actually. It was the church on the other side of town." But he said he'd think about it, and a couple of weeks later he rang us and said, "I will sell it to you." It was exactly the same amount of money we had to buy it, so we bought it.'

They converted it into a pottery studio and became self-taught potters – with a little help from their friends. 'Everyone from art school in Melbourne sent every potter they could think of up to visit. We had a string of about ten potters over the year who came up, one after the other, and had a great time. So we ended up being potters and we loved it.'

About seven years later they bought the St Bernard's building, another very old Catholic church, in nearby Batemans Bay. They moved it to Mogo on the back of two trucks. 'For some reason in those days, things didn't seem hard. We thought, We can do this, and it happened.' St Bernard's became their house. It was positioned about 50 metres behind the pottery studio and contained a large painting studio. 'It was a really big building and a big church, much bigger than St Mary's. A big weatherboard,' Vanessa said. Both church buildings were more than 120 years old. 'We are not religious at all. We've actually got two churches in the end and no religion.'

Mogo was a very different place back then. There was only a garage, a nursery and a general store, as well as their art studio. 'Absolutely nothing else was in town. Now you could say it's got about 56 businesses in the main street. It's gone from four to 56.'

As Mogo grew, it developed a real community vibe, which shifted again as it grew larger and more shops were added. It was a popular place. 'People would just come in and fall in love with the place and buy a property and set themselves up. I think they just liked the fact that they weren't in a major city or a major town.'

The art shop was also popular. Peter would paint large and vibrant landscapes and they'd produce colourful pottery. 'We could sell everything we made. It was a very successful business,' Vanessa said.

The end of 2019 was a busy time. It had been bone-dry for months. Everyone was talking about the fires. But it was Christmas time. Family were visiting. And Peter and Vanessa were hard at work making pots to sell during the January school holidays.

The Christmas spell was broken by an alert from the RFS on the morning of New Year's Eve telling them to evacuate. When fires had threatened their property in previous years, the couple had been assured by the firies at the time that their pottery building should be safe because there were a couple of fire hydrants right out the front of it. So Peter and Vanessa packed up some important things in their house and moved them to the apparent safety of the pottery studio. After that, they helped an elderly neighbour, transporting her to family in town.

And then it came.

'This fire was like a monster,' Vanessa said. 'It was two or three fires that had joined up. It was just so hot. It was 1200 or 1100 degrees Celsius. It was as hot as what we fire the kiln – almost. It was unbelievable.'

Both the pottery shed and the house were decimated.

'We didn't see it, luckily. Because I think we would have been a lot more distressed had we seen it. We went straight to stay with some friends on the coast and we stayed there all day, safe and waiting to hear what had happened. And then we heard in the afternoon that everything had burnt on our place. After that it was just sitting around trying to grasp the concept of having lost what we've lost.

'We went out the next morning and had a quick look. The road was closed and there was still a lot of smoke and burning trees around. The wires were down everywhere. It was just a mess. We couldn't hang around, it was too much to take in. Overwhelming. We alternated from devastated, a mess, to being positive for the future. Up and down.'

After our interview on the main street in Mogo, Peter and Vanessa took our film crew to their property. Peter told me it had been more than a home; it was a gem, he said. Theirs had been a magical existence. Incredibly, he pointed out a few pots that he hadn't yet finished in the kiln, which had ended up being fired in the inferno.

Yet Peter still had hope. 'I have a future,' he said. 'We are going to maybe start again. We are not sure yet. We will have a bit of rest time, recuperate, do a bit of grieving. We are just too raw at the moment, emotionally raw. I don't know if I have the energy to do it, but I'm going to try.'

When I spoke to the couple again a few months later, Vanessa said those first few days were numbing. 'It was disbelief, I guess. It hit me about two days later or three days later and then I was just distraught. You crash, you realise … you really realise what's happened.'

They ended up house-sitting for three weeks for a friend in Orange, 400 kilometres away. The distance proved vital. 'It was wonderful because it got us out of the smoke and the burning and the visuals,' Vanessa said. 'We started repairing, feeling better over there. Things started coming to us. People started contributing to a Go Fund Me online fundraiser that my daughter started.'

When they returned to the south coast, they were offered a small flat in Broulee to live in and a boatshed where Peter could paint. They were back creating art and making plans to set up a pop-up shop in Mogo where they and others would be able to sell their products. 'That gives us time to rebuild, which we are going to strive to do,' Vanessa said.

She and Peter were going to rebuild the pottery studio with a 'church-like' building. But not the house. 'We don't want to live in Mogo now. We can't really live there without being constantly reminded that we had this gorgeous building full of gorgeous things that we haven't got any more. But we can still work there, and we can be in a building which we can try and make as good as it was before it went, but we can't make the house anything like as good as it was.'

The delays waiting to rebuild were proving frustrating, as was the gaggle of tourists that were passing by to capture photos of their loss.

'Cleaning and sweeping and tidying is really therapeutic, but we can't do it because we are not allowed. We are not allowed in there, it's too dangerous,' Vanessa said. 'There's been a constant stream of people up at our place on the hill. Every time we go out to measure something, there's people thronging up there. They've come down to see what Mogo Pottery looks like all burnt down. I started off yelling at them. I said, "Look, there's nothing here for you. Why are you here?"' One of the tourists even stole the unfinished pots that had been fired during the blaze. 'It really upsets me, but I am getting used to it now.'

And they were painting, creating. Life was going on.

—

One of the things that people often talk about is that bushfire survivors should feel lucky because they got out with their lives.

Peter and Vanessa pointed out to me that when it happens to you, you realise that's wrong. The life they have now, the life they will have in the future, is not the same as the life they had before. Yes, they are alive. Yes, they are grateful to be alive. But they have lost the existence they had before this happened. Before I started to recognise that, I don't think I really understood the level of grief that people were feeling.

It was a profound realisation for me. As a society, as a culture, we are very optimistic and we like to think life goes on. And in many ways, it does. After the fires in the Snowy Mountains were contained, my dad was able to go back home. For most people in the Snowies it was a lucky escape. Life for them goes on. But it isn't that way for everyone. People like Margaret, Peter and Vanessa are actually trying to start a new life now.

And that's the challenge facing people affected by these fires right across Australia. They are having to reimagine what their life is. They may stay in their communities or they may move somewhere else. But wherever they are, many of them are having to start from scratch. They have to imagine a new version of their life. And they have to do that at the same time as grieving the one that they have lost.

Hamish Macdonald is the host of Q+A

Karen Michelmore is an ABC News journalist, writer and television producer

Where Are They Now?

Philippa McDonald

Throughout November 2019, almost 60 fires raged throughout New South Wales. Half of them were uncontained. The death toll was rising and nearly 500 homes destroyed.

On 17 November in the late-afternoon light, near Willawarrin not far from Kempsey on the mid-north coast of New South Wales, I looked out over a drought-stricken paddock alongside a dry riverbed and all I could see was a sea of dead cattle.

The carnage took my breath away. In the midst of it, I saw a man on a motorbike, his face and clothes dirty from the dust and ash. He wiped his eyes. 'They're the neighbours',' he said, pointing at the animals, which had been euthanised after being badly burnt in a fire. 'They'd been handfeeding for ages in this drought.'

Just a couple of kilometres from where we stood, a man had died trying to escape the flames. Barry Parsons had been living a reclusive life in a shed down the Kyuna Track with his two cats. In the hours before he was killed in the bushfires, 58-year-old Barry posted on Facebook: 'Seriously looks and sounds like apocalypse out there.'

How can a community come back from this? Drought meets bushfire, disaster upon disaster – and there was flooding and COVID-19 still to come.

Fast-forward five months and I'm again standing in that same paddock. As part of the Bushfire Recovery Reporting team I went back to the Willawarrin area where I'd felt so distressed for the farmers. I wanted to see for myself how they were going.

'Incomprehensible. I've never been so scared in all my life,' is how David Duff describes the firestorm that blazed through their property. 'Cost us about $1.2 million in about two hours. We were lucky to save the house.'

As their neighbour had told me months before, David and Carolyn Duff had been keeping their cattle alive by handfeeding in the weeks leading up to the fires. Ten weeks' worth of hay had cost $100,000. Then in a day it counted for nothing. Seventy head of cattle had to be euthanised. Six of their dogs were killed. Sixty kilometres of fencing were destroyed along with a shed full of essential farming machinery worth about $250,000.

Then in mid-January 2020 the Duffs received so much rain their property flooded.

'We've gone from hell to paradise in about six weeks,' David says. 'If you asked me probably prior to the rain, I wasn't in a real good spot. But our kids came to us and said, "Well, you can't give up, you're too young."'

Carolyn Duff did battle with the New South Wales government to receive an agricultural loan to keep six of their employees in work. 'Mentally,' she says, 'it is so tough.' After a five-month wait – and within 24 hours of appearing on ABC News – the money was deposited in the Duffs' bank account.

The ABC coverage of their story also had some unexpected results. Complete strangers got in touch with them. The Duffs were offered the use of a holiday house on the coast, and Carolyn was asked by a political party to run as a candidate in the next election.

In the months after the fires, the Duffs' modest cash flow had come from breeding Labradors. Following the puppies' TV premiere on the ABC, numerous requests came in about buying them, including one from the veteran broadcaster Mike Munro, who also offered a significant donation.

'Reckon if I had more puppies I could retire on them,' Carolyn says.

The Duffs are just one family among many hundreds who had their lives turned upside down by the fires. They know they are lucky that their house survived. Others did not have such luck.

Steve Williams documents the destruction to his house. (Philippa McDonald)

A temporary accommodation 'pod' arrives at Louise Richardson's block, Hickey's Creek, NSW. (Philippa McDonald)

—

Steve Williams had the face of a haunted man, dark soulful eyes and a big grey beard. We first met in Batemans Bay on Sunday, 5 January 2020. The sky was a vivid orange, the air thick with smoke, and ash was falling from the sky.

The area was still under threat from the fires. I'd spent much of the previous day and evening on Long Beach where dozens of locals were congregating on the beach with their boats, ready to take to the bay in the event of another onslaught. Fresh in everyone's mind were those who had taken refuge on the beach at Malua Bay as houses and the local bowlo incinerated and fire roared on nearby headlands and in the streets.

The combination of heat and the dangerous forecast winds had everyone on edge. During my 6 pm cross that Saturday night, the temperature suddenly dropped from searing dry heat to chilly, and enormous gusts of wind became gale force. Fortunately, that time, for this community, the wind was not on the side of the fires.

The next morning Hamish Macdonald and producer Antonette Collins told me that I just had to meet Steve Williams. With communications and power down I ended up knocking on his motel door.

Steve was still in shock. He has emphysema and diabetes, and on New Year's Eve 2019 he escaped to the beach with just the clothes on his back. 'It went up,' he said of the way his house burnt, 'from being like a candle, to throwing a cup of petrol on it and then seconds later like someone threw a drum of petrol on it. The house just exploded.'

The ferocity and the intensity of the fire destroyed half of the homes in his Catalina cul-de-sac. 'There's seven houses here just totalled. Emptiness, I can't describe it. There's just nothing there.'

The kitchen table and the barbecue were a twisted mess and the esky had melted, the remnants of the Christmas ham still in it.

'So what am I going to do I don't know, as in accommodation,' he said. 'There'll be no accommodation around here for a long time.'

There was no way he would live next to bushland again, he said. 'It's too emotional for me.'

At 72, Steve had been through life's ups and downs. I asked him where this particular crisis sat and Steve took a deep breath. 'Agh, I would say it's pretty high on the chart, it's probably number one.'

Like the Duffs, Steve was the recipient of enormous generosity after his story went to air on the ABC. Several people got in touch offering him free accommodation and he moved to Sydney. 'I was up there for a bit over a month,' he tells me when I check back in with him months later. 'Jackie and Keith were a beautiful couple.'

He spent some time living in motels, and then a woman from Wollongong helped him look for a home. 'She got me to pull my finger out and do something,' he says. 'She was absolutely terrific helping me.'

Eight months on Steve has found a place back in Batemans Bay. 'Right behind me is the bush, but I feel a little bit more comfortable, it's more heavily populated. But if I smelt bushfires, I'd panic. I'm dreading New Year's Eve, I think that's going to be a hard day to take.'

Steve is now contemplating a move to Queensland and he has taken up his favourite hobby of crocheting again. 'My grandmother taught me when I was six and I love it.'

—

Time and again as I have reported on the bushfires, I've been struck by how life can change in an instant. How you can go from living on your block in the bush, surrounded by the stuff of life, to losing it all in one horrific afternoon. This is what happened to Louise Richardson, a 60-year-old disability support worker, when a fireball jumped the river at Hickeys Creek and destroyed everything on her block.

After the fire, Louise and her husband, Keith, and their teenage son, Calum, set up a small caravan on their block, 40 kilometres inland from Kempsey. They strung up a tarpaulin over an outside kitchen where they have a kettle, a small stove and fridge. They also sometimes stay with their neighbours.

In the Kempsey shire where they live, 40 per cent of the land was burnt in the bushfires and 67 homes were lost.

Louise and Keith had been 'building up' their home over the past 30 years. 'It was just a family place that everyone came to, everyone popped in,' Louise tells me, when I meet her five months after the fire. She's only just got the water back on.

On the day of the fire, she'd driven into town to pick up the grandkids to take them home for the weekend, and was on her way back to Hickeys Creek when Keith rang and told her to turn around and stay in Kempsey.

'I knew it was pretty bad,' she recalls. 'We couldn't get home that night.'

It was to be another 24 hours before Louise would hear that her son, Calum, and husband, Keith, were all right. They'd escaped to a neighbour's place. 'When a councilwoman told me she had just seen a boy chasing a dog, I cried,' Louise says. 'I knew that they'd both be OK.'

—

You get to Louise's 30-acre block down a series of unsealed roads and a winding dirt track. It's almost subtropical and would have been beautiful before the fires, but the trees are trying to bounce back. In what was once the family's front garden are the broken and molten remnants of their life before the November bushfires: burnt bicycles, flower pots, sculptures, knick-knacks, china, an iron surround for an open fire. There's even an old Singer sewing machine on its side. Louise has laid stones around these once-cherished items, creating a memorial to the past.

'When everyone was all right, nothing else mattered,' Louise says of how she felt once she learnt Keith and Calum were safe. 'It just didn't matter that everything is gone. I'm still a bit that way.'

They didn't have insurance, so charities and government have lent a helping hand with a series of grants to get by. 'We'll get there, we always do.'

The day I meet Louise, something is due to arrive that will make life a little bit easier: a small rectangular lifeline in the form of a temporary accommodation 'pod'. It's a 17-square-metre shipping container with mod cons: a toilet, shower, kitchen and 2,300-litre water tank.

'Oh, that's going to be great,' Louise says. 'There's going to be running water. It's got everything we need. We can actually move home. It's just so good.'

The next morning a convoy of trucks rolls into a council holding bay in Kempsey, where, with military precision, the pod is lifted by a crane onto a flat-topped truck.

I am back at Louise's and watch in awe as this huge truck comes down her narrow driveway, and within 20 minutes a crane is lowering a shipping container down onto a cleared block. Louise, Keith and Calum are there too and they began to smile, cheer and clap.

As soon as the converted shipping container is balanced and anchored onto the block, Louise steps up and into her new home.

'It's got everything, it's such a relief,' she says. 'It's just going to make life so much easier. It's making it more like home again.'

The New South Wales government and the Minderoo Foundation are providing 200 of these pods to people across the state. Bushfire-affected residents can live in them for up to two years.

'Hopefully, by then we'll have another house; that's what I'm hoping,' Louise tells me, beaming.

—

Almost two and a half thousand homes were destroyed in the bushfires that burnt from August to February. Thousands were displaced and had to live in emergency accommodation or with family and friends. Complete strangers reached out with a helping hand and it might be years before some have a permanent place to call home.

Tina Hag was at home with two-month-old baby Edward, two-year-old Nora, four-year-old Villiam and six-year-old Jesse when the firestorm tore through the centre of the New South Wales town of Rappville, just south of Casino, engulfing their rented home. She managed to get the kids in the car and flee with just the family photos.

'I just think about what could have happened,' Tina tells me. 'It's pretty scary. I think every day how lucky we were to get out of there.'

In their small north coast community, two people were killed and 14 homes were lost along with the town's biggest employer, a timber mill.

The family are now living in a shed, rent-free, 50 kilometres away from Rappville. The owner lives overseas and says they can have it for as long as they need it. It's a lifeline but it's far from easy.

'It's harder now than it was in the beginning,' Robert Collier, Tina's partner, tells me. 'It's just been so long. It's a struggle being in the same room all the time, putting the kids to sleep, no plumbing inside.'

Life in the shed at Ellangowan has been far from stress-free, and summer brought some terrifying moments. Their temporary home was also in the line of fire. The family had to evacuate twice as the Bora Ridge fire came close.

'I thought, here we go again,' Robert says. 'Burnt leaves raining down, you could hear the fire roaring.'

The shed is on the top of a hill and it's now the middle of winter when we speak. Temperatures here in winter dip below zero. In summer, it reaches the high 30s. Luckily, Robert is an air-conditioning specialist, so he's installed heating in the shed, but it's crowded in the small same space and they have to go outside for running water.

Tina and Robert are now saving up to build a new home on a block of land they've bought in Rappville, where another house burnt down. Despite the distance, they are still sending their older children to the Rappville Public School, which was literally a lifeline for the community of 200 people during the crisis.

'It became an impromptu evacuation centre,' principal Kathleen Collis tells me. 'Fifty to 100 people sheltered here, plus the animals they could bring with them.'

Those seeking refuge at the school used the hoses and extinguishers to put out spot fires, but then the power went out and they had to rely on a local fire brigade for protection. Homes and buildings all around the school were wiped out in the fire.

'I would not wish that upon anyone ever again,' Kathleen says. 'It would have been very traumatic for them. The scars will be felt for years.'

In the days and weeks following the fires, the school distributed hamper packs, provided support for wellbeing activities and opened up their facilities for showers 'because running water wasn't happening'. Kathleen says the children are going OK. 'They're very resilient. They bounce back really well.'

Tina Hag and her baby outside the family's damaged house in Rappville, NSW. (Bellinda Kontimonas/ABC)

Rappville Primary School, a phoenix rising from the ashes. (Philippa McDonald)

Kathleen says she's 'super proud' of the school community, and it's one she knows well. As a child, she went to the very school she now runs. She lives locally and her family farm was also affected by the fires. Three hundred and twenty acres burnt and they lost 60 per cent of their livestock. But Kathleen tells me there is hope on the horizon. A few calves have been born, and the kids are giving them names like Sparkie, Cinders and Coals.

Standing in front of Rappville Public School, it's hard to miss the massive freshly painted mural – a phoenix looming large, wings outstretched, rising from the ashes.

'The community wanted something that was uplifting and fitting for what we'd all experienced,' Kathleen says. 'We've got a marvellous phoenix, which stands pride of place in the centre of our school building and it says on each side, "We will rise."

'And that's what we're doing – bit by bit, day by day, step by step, we are rising.'

—

The impact of the bushfires is being felt deeply still. There are those who paid the ultimate price, those who were injured, those who lost everything, and those who count themselves, their family and neighbours lucky to be alive.

The ferocity of these seemingly unstoppable fires shocked the nation. They created their own treacherously unpredictable weather events.

Communities who thought they were safe could do little to defend their homes against fires that bore down with barely any warning. Hundreds huddled together on beaches, while others jumped into lakes, treading water until the emergency passed. It was indeed a fight for survival.

Other communities were on edge for months as nearby fires burnt deep in inaccessible areas of national park. They watched as the red glow on the horizon kept creeping closer, eventually unleashing a destructive fury upon them.

In the course of my reporting, I have met people who were evacuated five times over the space of a couple weeks, and people who slept in their car or camped out at the local evacuation centre with their 90-year-old mum, not knowing whether their home would be still standing when they returned. Nothing in Australia's peacetime history matches the scale of the evacuation. Nursing-home residents were evacuated and thousands of tourists were directed to leave the New South Wales south coast.

For tens of thousands of firefighters who battled relentlessly in the hottest conditions on record, there was little reprieve even in the middle of the night when temperatures usually dip.

Firefighters lost their lives: Australians and three Americans who came to lend a hand. Even the toughest RFS leaders described their deaths as a 'horrendous kick in the guts'.

The loss of precious wildlife was huge – three billion and still counting – reminding us of the fragility and vulnerability of our environment.

Inquiries and a Royal Commission have told us we must prepare for 'the new extreme', a future where there are more natural disasters and the time for action is now.

We've been told the recovery is a 'marathon' and still an aspiration for many, but as the months roll in to a year, rebuilding is starting to happen. For some, recovery means leaving, moving on to start a new life somewhere far away.

Trauma comes in waves and some have been going it alone and are now only just coming forward to get help.

In the tough times, Australians step up. There's been a huge outpouring of generosity, hundreds of millions of dollars has been donated and distributed to help those in need.

While it will never make the headlines, the kindness of strangers has made a big difference to so many who never thought they'd be homeless.

In the most terrible of times, the Commissioner of Resilience NSW, Shane Fitzsimmons, sums it up best: 'In our most harrowing of times, we saw an unparalleled rising of the human spirit.'

During 2019 and 2020, Philippa McDonald covered the bushfires and bushfire recovery for the ABC

Kangaroo Island, 11 January 2020.
(Brittany Evins/ABC)

The New Normal

Josh Szeps

'GOATS!', MY FRIEND'S DAD, A SIXTY-SOMETHING TOWN planner, announced, jabbing the air with a forkful of watermelon and feta.

We were perched next to each other on his sofa, sweaty thighs too close. A Christmas lunch. 'Put goats in the national parks,' he explained to me. 'They eat everything. No more fuel on the ground! Nature's firefighters, they call them.'

This was supposed to have been a barbie, but had been downgraded to an indoor huddle. That was happening a lot in late 2019. Outdoor events were being cancelled to escape the ashy chowder that hung where the sky used to be.

I glanced at Sweaty-Thighed Town Planner's wife, a cheerful suicide therapist. I wondered, as she reached for a big glass of sauvignon blanc, if maybe this wasn't the first time she'd heard him discuss the Miraculous Goat Solution. 'Who calls them “nature’s firefighters”, darling?’ she asked, sipping hungrily.

He shot me a look that said he was being interrogated by a rooster. ‘The people who don’t want to get burnt down by bloody bushfires, honey.’

‘Well, I don’t know about that,’ she said. ‘What I do know is that we’re going to remember this summer.’ She paused and put her glass down. Suddenly, violently, she shook her head, as if to reset her face from despondency to cheer. She smiled hard. Her eyes were tired. ‘We’re going to remember this summer,’ she repeated. ‘Forever.’

—

It was when a water-bombing helicopter fell out of the sky that I first took notice.

That was November 13th, west of Brisbane. Huge swathes of Queensland had already been evacuated, from Bundaberg to the Gold Coast. There had even been a quaint, Dunkirkian rescue of Sunshine Coast residents in small ferries. The media treated this as a feel-good yarn, like one of those stories at the end of the news about penguins having sex. Those kooky Queenslanders and their maritime escapades! What vim! What vigour! What pluck!

Just eight weeks later, another maritime rescue would book-end the most horrendous natural disaster in living memory. The navy's biggest ship, a machine-gun-clad, quarter-kilometre-long assault vessel, would be deployed to the orange-aired hellscape of the New South Wales south coast. You wouldn't have believed it in November. Things were different then. We were different then.

There'd been some warnings. In October, Michael Mann, one of the world's most prominent climate scientists (and one of the fathers of the 'hockey stick' graph showing the acceleration in global warming), told me on ABC Radio Sydney that Australia is uniquely vulnerable to climate chaos. Our dryness and heat put us at greater risk than arguably any other rich country.

Six months before that, Greg Mullins, a former New South Wales fire chief, had convened more than 20 ex-emergency chiefs from around Australia to warn the government about worsening bushfire conditions due to climate change. They requested a meeting with Prime Minister Scott Morrison in April. The PM declined. They asked again after he won re-election in May. He declined again.

By the time the chopper crashed into a bushfire on the Darling Downs in November, there were 80-odd fires raging in Queensland. There were about 60 more in New South Wales. Winds were strong. Temperatures were high. Sydney's fire danger rating was raised to an all-new level: 'catastrophic'.

For most city slickers, though, it was still theoretical. It was headlines in the papers and footage on TV.

Until the smoke.

—

Summers in Sydney are brilliant. Literally, brilliant. Brilliantly bright, brilliantly blue. Ablaze with sparkling waters and distant skies.

The Black Summer was not. It was beige. The sky deflated over a dead, pastel world. Sydney was as soupy as a sauna and as fragrant as an ashtray. The Harbour Bridge looked like it'd been Photoshopped onto the English moors.

On December 10th, Sydneysiders awoke to a total white-out. All ferry services were cancelled. You couldn't see the end of the street, let alone across the water. Office workers were evacuated as fire alarms went berserk. At Bondi Beach, 70 kilometres from the fire front, cars had their headlights on. Ash settled on windscreens. People bought masks.

I was working seven days a week. On ABC TV, I co-anchored *Weekend Breakfast.* On radio, I presented the weekday breakfast show. Every morning at 3.30 when my alarm went off, I could tell how bad the fires were just from the smell. I'd tiptoe over squeaky floorboards in the pre-dawn dark. I'd stop at the door of my two-year-old twins' bedroom. Often, one would be coughing.

I'd drive to work, cursing the wiper fluid for running out (yet again! I need to refill it, again), peering through charred streaks, recalling some statistic about how many cigarettes' worth of smoke we were all inhaling every day. Was it 15 cigarettes? Forty cigarettes? Tiny, two-year-old lungs. Did it matter?

A radio studio is a spaceship, perfectly insulated. But as the atmosphere thickened, the studios started reeking. Toxins got in and couldn't get out. The thick air caught in my throat. I was interviewing from a compromised spaceship; a cocoon worse than what it was cocooned from.

Let's pause for a sec.

I know how frivolous it is to whine about smoke while, in the bush, houses were exploding and people were dying. But it's impossible to understand the crisis without understanding its most widespread physical effect.

What millions upon millions of people felt, day after day, week after week, was not the heat of the flames but the raspy throats, the itchy eyes, the whited-out skies, the lazy flakes of ash settling on clotheslines, the children languishing impatiently inside. That firey smell everywhere, that smoker's cough. The wheezing. It just went on and on and on. Who wants to live in a city like that? If this were to happen every year, what would you do? How many summers would you put up with it? How long until you left the city for good?

It's portentous, in hindsight, that this was how we entered 2020. A year that will forever be a byword for covering your face, for staying inside. Months before the air carried viral pathogens, it carried microparticles of burnt leaves, burnt animals, burnt homes, burnt bones. How quaint that we lived for decades not needing masks, and then, when we did, we suddenly needed them twice. The macro and the micro, the flames and the germs.

Mark Twain supposedly said that history doesn't repeat itself, but it often rhymes. What a dark rhyme 2020 turned out to be.

—

By early January, the fires were the biggest news story in the world. Britain's *The Times*, the *Daily Telegraph*, *The Guardian* and the *Financial Times*, Toronto's *Globe and Mail*, and the *New York Times* all ran the same photo on their front page, of a kangaroo bounding past an inferno.

The fires were so large they were creating their own weather systems. Hundreds of millions of tonnes of smoke created pyrocumulus clouds that formed supercell thunderstorms, generating dry lightning that started yet more fires. Tornadoes tossed trucks aside and blew apart buildings. In South America, sunsets glowed red with Aussie soot. NASA released satellite images of smoke plumes circumnavigating the planet, drifting around the globe and back to their birthplace like some deranged cosmic salmon swimming home.

I sat at the desk in the ABC TV studio and clenched my teeth. Live on air, a senator was explaining to me that the federal government was doing everything asked of it by the states and territories because, as I may not understand, under Australia's federal system, emergency management is a responsibility of the states and territories, and the federal government was doing everything being asked of it by the states and territories which, as he'd mentioned, are responsible for emergency management under Australia's federal system, so, really, thus forth and hencely, we should all, in fact, be really satisfied – really, reeeally grateful, ackchyually – for the government's contribution to something that really wasn't, constitutionally speaking, its problem, *quod erat demonstrandum.*

The public didn't buy it.

We'd reached a tipping point. You could feel it. I heard it every day from listeners who were exhausted; emotionally brutalised. On the telly, I interviewed reporters standing under skies as dark as night in the middle of a summer's day. Landscapes of blood-red air.

I was tired. I was frayed. I was afraid, too, for my toddlers, for what would become of us all. Later, much later, a lifetime later (by which I mean two months), when the pandemic derailed the world like a slow-motion train crash, I never felt as fearful as during the fires. Coronavirus felt like a one-off. The firestorm felt like it might become a new normal: the first cycle of some endless, annual, suicidal opera.

—

On January 2nd, presenting *Breakfast* on ABC Radio Sydney, I channelled the audience's frustration in an improvised editorial that went viral. The federal government was still insisting it was doing everything asked of it by the states. My response was six minutes long. It included these remarks:

> Sydneysiders are exhausted. We are weary. We're over it. We're just over it. I have a Japanese friend who said: 'When there's an earthquake or a typhoon that causes this level of damage, the Japanese army is in there like a shot.' Same in the UK. When there are floods, in goes the army.
>
> No one's suggesting that we ought to do that on an ad hoc, knee-jerk basis right now – suddenly send in the troops and cause all kinds of kerfuffles where they're not needed or wanted or useful. But how is it that we're not thinking carefully about setting up a system in which our response is coordinated federally? In which we throw everything at this? If this were a foreign invader doing this, if it were a terrorist attack causing this kind of hardship, what would we be doing?

And I added:

> This is not a partisan political issue. It's not Scott Morrison's fault that there are fires. I'm not blaming

> anyone. But I am channelling a sense I'm getting that's building up; building up too much to ignore any more. It's a sense of a loss of leadership, a loss of faith, a loss of vision, a loss of being up to the seriousness of the challenge.
>
> Why aren't we buying every rusty old Hercules plane that's sitting on a military airfield in every poor country in the world that wants to sell it? … Have we asked the Americans and the Canadians for every spare plane that can be refitted? What are the limitations here? Are there not enough airfields? Have we commandeered every private airstrip in the state? … If this were World War Two, we would find a way. Are we serious? … This has been going on for a while. Are. We. Serious?

Not the most eloquent soliloquy that's ever graced the airwaves, but it hit a nerve. The following morning, I interviewed Greg Mullins, the ex-fire boss whose warnings about extreme bushfire weather had been ignored.

I wanted him to cool me down with some bland managerial expertise, but he was angrier than I was.

> **MULLINS:** Our prime minister should be … ringing around countries like France, Portugal, Spain, Canada, that have all these purpose-built, water-scooping aircraft … The ADF [Australian Defence Forces] are

dying to help. But the national government says they're not needed.

SZEPS: Is there a logistical impediment why that is impossible? Do we not have enough pilots? Are there not enough airstrips?

MULLINS: The logistical impediments are the purse strings in Canberra.

SZEPS: If you're right, then that is absolutely and totally shameful. And not just shameful, but a political non-starter. I hope you're wrong. I hope you're overly cynical. I haven't done a poll in the field, Greg, but I am absolutely certain that if you polled Australians … there would be very, very few people who'd say we should allow these fires to burn one second longer than is necessary, or burn an additional single square kilometre, because we don't want to spend money on it.

MULLINS: Well, I can hear you being a bit angry. And I'm furious. Because that IS the case.

The next day, the prime minister reversed course and decided it was a national responsibility after all. He announced $20 million to lease firefighting aircraft and called in the army for the first time in Australian history.

—

As the fire conditions deteriorated, so did the quality of the national conversation.

'Firebugs fuelling crisis as national arson toll hits 183,' a headline in *The Australian* newspaper said. It wasn't true. That figure of 183 included every fire offence since the beginning of 2019, including such high crimes as operating a campsite barbie without a permit. The authorities made it clear that firebugs hadn't been a significant factor in starting any of the major fires.

Didn't matter. The Liberal senator Concetta Fierravanti-Wells tweeted that 87 per cent of bushfires were man-made. She stood in the Senate and hinted darkly that the arsonists may be part of 'a sinister collective, conducting eco-terrorism'.

The Australian later qualified the arson claim, but not before it went global. Donald Trump Jr retweeted it. Media hacks fanned it. Fox News host Tomi Lahren editorialised in the United States: 'The fact of the matter is this: Australia has an arson problem you can't pin on global warming, climate change, or whatever title you're giving your environmental boogeyman these days.'

While some were blaming arson, others were calling for more of it. The New South Wales Shooters, Fishers and Farmers Party introduced a bill to allow farmers to start fires in national parks. This was part of a broader narrative, pushed by radio hacks and tabloid columnists, that the fires were the fault of the Greens for preventing hazard-reduction burns. Certainly, hazard-reduction burns are a crucial tool in bushfire prevention. But New South Wales had been ruled by a pragmatic conservative government for nearly a decade and had conducted over 137,000 hectares of hazard-reduction burns in the previous year alone.

But if hazard reduction wasn't to blame, maybe cows were. Or the lack of cows? The New South Wales agriculture minister called for grazing in national parks to help manage fuel loads. The environment minister from his own party slapped him down. 'Cows can't stop bushfires', the headline in the *Sydney Morning Herald* helpfully explained.

The CSIRO, Australia's peak science body, went further, suggesting that grazing could make things worse. Dry shrubs are flammable and wildflowers aren't. Cows eat the juicy flowers and drag the shrubs around, spreading the fuel load. 'There is no evidence that either logging or cattle grazing reduces the risk of fire in forest environments,' stated the National Parks Association of New South Wales.

So why were some commentators so fixated on hazard burns, national park grazing, and arson? Because those explanations shared one virtue: they weren't climate change.

'When are we going to wake up and stop using this as an excuse to justify the climate change hoax,' Alan Jones, Australia's most influential broadcaster, roared. His Sky News colleague Rowan Dean railed about the 'loonies in the climate cult'.

Sure, the Australian Academy of Science said human-induced climate change was worsening extreme weather events. Sure, the Australian weather bureau said climate change was influencing the frequency and severity of bushfire conditions. Sure, NASA agreed. Sure, the CSIRO agreed.

But if those pointy-headed nerds were right, then the commentators who'd spent years bamboozling their audiences with nit-picky climate chicanery now had blood on their hands. They needed the climate to be irrelevant. What would it say about them if it wasn't?

The same conundrum partly explained the prime minister's haplessness. Morrison wasn't a climate denier, but he was a proud booster of the coal industry and an equally proud pooh-pooher of carbon pricing. Besides, climate policy had brought down more than one Aussie leader in the past decade. Morrison wanted no part of it. He dodged climate questions with the elegance of a wounded bull.

His poll numbers sank. He'd taken a mistimed family holiday to Hawaii in December. When he hurried back to Australia to visit fire-ravaged communities, he was heckled by locals. Footage showed a woman refusing to shake his hand, only to have him grab her hand and forcibly shake it. When he was at the fires, he looked opportunistic. When he wasn't, he looked neglectful. The poor guy couldn't win.

—

The Saturday before Australia Day, the skies finally opened. Sydney had its biggest single-day rainfall in four months. The day after that, a man disembarked at Melbourne Airport from Guangdong. He was Australia's first confirmed coronavirus case.

In that single weekend, in two consecutive days, January 18th and 19th, Australia transitioned from the beginning of the end of one national trauma to the beginning of the beginning of another.

This time, Morrison didn't blink. Australia's initial response to the pandemic was among the most effective in the world. In contrast to the buck-passing on the bushfires, the PM created a national cabinet to coordinate state and federal response. Rather than downplaying the problem, he launched a full-scale mobilisation: border closures, quarantine, physical distancing, mass testing, tracing and isolation. Instead of dismissing expert opinion, he deferred to it. In the flames of the bushfires, a leader had been forged.

There's an old Zen parable about a farmer whose horse runs away. His neighbours all say, 'How terrible,' and he just says, 'We'll see.' The next day, the horse returns, bringing three wild horses with it. 'How wonderful!' the neighbours say. The old man says, 'We'll see.' The farmer's son tries to tame the horses but gets thrown and breaks his leg. The neighbours say, 'How terrible!' and the farmer says, 'We'll see.' The next day, military officers come door to door to conscript all able-bodied young males to fight. They leave behind the son with the broken leg. The neighbours say, 'How wonderful!'

And the farmer says, 'We'll see.'

As early as December 2019, countries all over the world were being seeded with the mysterious new virus. As Europeans went Christmas shopping, as Americans drank warm wine at office holiday parties, SARS-CoV-2 was spilling silently out of planes and rippling through their populations.

In Australia, meanwhile, international travellers were cancelling their trips in droves. The flames were a firewall against the epidemiological inferno abroad. Australia was forced into self-isolation before we'd even heard the term. The tourism industry was crushed. How terrible, we all said.

We'll see.

—

I drove to Cronulla Beach in early February. The sky was deep blue. It smelled like summer again, the brilliant kind.

I was getting lunch with Michael Mann, the climate scientist. He'd just been on ABC TV's *Q+A*, the first episode of the year. We chatted about the fires, politics, the future. As we finished lunch and stood up, I told him about my friend's dad at the party. The goats in the national park. The wife who said we'd remember this summer forever.

'We will, won't we,' I said, as we stepped outside. 'We're going to remember this summer forever.'

'That's not what scares me,' Mann said. He inhaled deeply and gazed towards the ocean, the waves pounding the shore. 'What scares me,' he said, 'is that we might get used to it.'

Josh Szeps is a presenter on ABC Radio Sydney and a former host of ABC TV's Weekend Breakfast. *His podcast is* Uncomfortable Conversations with Josh Szeps.

Kosciuszko National Park,
8 January 2020. (Matt Roberts/ABC)

Acknowledgements

The contributors wish to thank everyone who shared their time and stories at what was an extremely difficult time.

Brittany Evins: This story wouldn't have been possible without the help of Trent Murphy and the entire ABC Adelaide team. Thank you for your guidance and support. Thanks also to the other incredible people who shared their experiences, that weren't mentioned here. Your stories will never be forgotten. Lastly but not least to my beautiful family and support network at home.

Nick Hose: thanks to David Berthold, Daniel Saward, Justin Stevens and the good folks of Batlow for trusting us with their story.

Melinda James: special mention to Jen Courtney, producer extraordinaire at ABC Illawarra, as well as to all my other super dedicated and talented ABC Illawarra colleagues; Superintendent Mark Williams from RFS Shoalhaven for always being unflappable and available whatever the hour; and ABC listeners for their vast knowledge, empathy and willingness to help one another.

Jonathon Kendall: thanks to Leo op den Brouw, as well as Victoria Police, Parks Victoria, the Australian Defence Force including the helicopter crew that got us from Gabo; my family and my wife, Belinda, who is always as cool as a cucumber in a crisis.

Jennifer McCutcheon: thanks to my amazing ABC colleagues, who gave up so much to work around the clock to help keep people safe during the summer.

Philippa McDonald: thanks to Sally Bryant from Legal Aid NSW, Susan Cullinan and Angela Lemme from Australian Red Cross, Resilience NSW, David Crust from NPWS NSW, Ben Shepherd from NSW Rural Fire Service, Mayor Liz Campbell from Kempsey Shire Council, and Mayor Carol Sparks from Glen Innes Severn Council.

Greg Nelson: thanks to the volunteer firefighters of the NSW RFS, the communities of the NSW south coast and staff of ABC News, ABC South East and *7.30*. Indefatigable all.

Baz Ruddick: thanks to Jack Wotton.

Josh Szeps: thanks to Paul Barry and the Hon. Matt Kean, MP, for their generosity in sharing their research.

Claire Wheaton: thanks to the Redmond Family and Yannis Gantner.

Copyright

Claire Wheaton's stories © Claire Wheaton 2021
The Smell of Smoke © Erin Semmler 2021
The Fire Near Me © Richard Glover 2021
The Faces of Fire © Brittany Evins 2021
Currowan on the Run © Jessie Davies 2021
One, Two, Three, Breathe © Adriane Reardon 2021
Dark Days © Philip Williams and Greg Nelson 2021
Battling On © Casey Briggs 2021
Disaster Unfolds Live On Air © Melinda James 2021
A Black Horizon © Jonathon Kendall 2021
Escape from the Flames © Jade Macmillan 2021
Displaced © Matthew Doran 2021
Escape to the Jetty © Stacey Lee 2021
The Black Ops Brigade © Matthew Doran 2021
The Clean-up © Tom Joyner 2021
Courageous Women © Philippa McDonald 2021
Dispatched Far and Wide © Jennifer McCutcheon 2021
Emergency Services © Daniel Doody 2021
The Battle for Batlow © Nick Hose 2021
Building Community in a Scorched Summer © Baz Ruddick 2021
A Place Like Home © Hamish Macdonald and Karen Michelmore 2021
Where Are They Now? © Philippa McDonald 2021
The New Normal © Josh Szeps 2021